SPIRIT WORLD AND SPIRIT LIFE

SPIRIT WORLD AND SPIRIT LIFE

Descriptions received through the automatic writing of Charlotte Elizabeth Dresser (C.E.D.)

Edited by

Fred Rafferty ("F. R.")

www.whitecrowbooks.com

Spirit World and Spirit Life

Original copyright © 1922 by Fred Raffrerty, Santa Ana, California.
This copyright © 2025 by White Crow Productions Ltd. All rights reserved.
Published by White Crow Books, an imprint of White Crow Productions Ltd.

A CIP catalogue record for this book is available from the British Library.
For information, contact White Crow Books by e-mail: info@whitecrowbooks.com.

Cover Design by Astrid@Astridpaints.com
Interior design by Velin@Perseus-Design.com

Paperback: ISBN: 9781786772961
eBook: ISBN: 9781786772978

Non-Fiction / BODY, MIND & SPIRIT / Afterlife & Reincarnation

www.whitecrowbooks.com

PREFACE

~

SEVENTEEN years ago, when quite alone, after the 'passing' of father, mother, sister, and brothers, I formed a friendship, that grew into a companionship so fine that the world became for me a happier place and life a brighter thing. We were a trio: 'Dee,' 'F.R.,' and 'Sis'; for so we changed our names to familiar and intimate expression.

Twelve years passed, with no break in the happy association, and then suddenly and with little warning Dee passed out of this earthly life. To me, remained the hope of renewing the companionship in a world where parting is unknown. To. F. R. a black wall, beyond which, nothing! For, long before, his mind had accepted the reasoning of materialistic philosophy, and, arguing from that standpoint, death ended all; and life, going out like a spent candle, could in nowise be relighted.

Months went by. Finally a few friends, interested in psychic phenomena, asked us to join them in experiment.

From the first, even through primitive table-tipping and the much criticized Ouija-board, messages came that arrested the attention, and F. R. grew more and more interested. Later, through Ouija, I was asked to try automatic writing; and, after a few trials, found the pencil moving quite freely and giving messages which I could not have anticipated, and which many times were quite contrary to my own thought and belief.

Dee almost at first gave her name and proved to us her identity. Mary—Mary Bosworth—Dee has told us, is the good angel who was sent to meet her as she passed into the Beyond. Mary is the leader of the communicating circle on that side.

With this explanation or introduction, I have left the work of selecting and editing the mass of material coming through the pencil, to the patient care of F. R.

'Sis.'

CONTENTS

~

1

INTRODUCTORY

~

T HE reasons for the publication of this book may be inferred from the various communications recorded in this chapter. They were not all given at one time, but are fragments from many conversations and messages, placed together because belonging to one subject.

"Give the truth to the world, let it be received where it will. Many will read the messages. Some will accept the truth, others will read through curiosity, a few will ridicule. Yet to all is the truth given, and to all remains the power of choice.

"The hope of the world in this time of trouble is in spiritualizing all forms of activity. Love and service; service and love. These must be the watchwords if the world is to come into lasting peace. We are trying to influence a world that is going astray and might cause undreamed-of suffering. We are trying to overcome the thought of materialists and to bring a spiritual outlook into the earthly life. We need the help of all on earth who can think in spiritual terms. The great battle to be fought now is between the spiritual and the material, between idealism and carnalism. I have received instructions from the higher powers to call all who will to help. You can help by giving the world our thought,

1

and I am asking that you help because the battle will be long and the victory far away."

"You do not realize the necessity in your world for a stronger and more compelling spiritual belief. We think it possible to create that belief through the influence and teachings from this side. We are trying to exert a power for good upon a world that sadly needs our help. All influences for good are needed. For many the church is sufficient; for some a future life must be absolutely proved; others require manifestations or messages from the unseen world. But beyond these are the few who seek the larger field of spiritual truth. All ways are needed, if through them we can teach the earth-people that they are now, through their mortal lives, preparing either happiness or bitter regret or sorrow, for the future life. The thoughts, actions, [and] habits of that life extend their influence to this one. Lives filled with evil deeds, injustice, impurity, cruelty, dishonesty, cannot wash themselves clean by slipping out of the material body through that which you call death. Make it known, you who can see and tell it to others. Make it known to all who will learn!"

"Do you understand how different life would be there if all would try to give as well as to receive; if all would learn to serve unselfishly the world in which they live, and learn the higher happiness of spiritual thought and life? The coming of the new age is not for one or for two to bring in, but rather the mighty influence from here moving through the spiritually discerning ones there."

At one time this word was sent through the pencil: "When I saw myself—saw the mistakes, the wrong thinking and wrong doing of my earthly life, the revelation filled me with dismay. It is this last discerning of our own earthly lives that fulfills the old teaching of the 'judgment day.' Remember that every good act, every loving, unselfish service, is registered upon the spirit and helps to prepare a brighter future for the soul when it arrives here. Why will the earth people be so blind? How can we emphasize more strongly the truth, that mortals are preparing their future lives now, and that their heavenly state is for them to choose? Make it plainly known that selfishness embodies all other sins, for it is the yielding to self-love and self-indulgence that creates other sins."

2

"We were all mistaken on earth, ministers and laymen alike. Lawyers are not just; merchants not honest; business men forgetting their honor while grasping greater gains; ministers allowing creeds to outweigh service. Why do clergymen emphasize creed instead of service? Why do they mourn over death, instead of telling of the wonderful opportunities beyond? Why do judges punish crime instead of educating the criminal? Why does the world spend its care and thought on the fleeting shadows of earth life, rather than study the conditions of the heavenly one which is to last forever?"

"You tell us that the world does not believe the messages from here because of the false teaching that comes to earth from those pretending to be heavenly guides. It is true that many undeveloped and mischievous ones on this plane are sending false and foolish teaching to whoever will receive it there. Yet, does the world abandon religion because of its grievous errors? Do teachers stop teaching because ignorant ones put forward wrong ideas? Do honest men give up their honest business because dishonest ones are busy in graft or robbery? Do physicians stop healing the sick because of the unlearned pretenders in their profession? Good and evil have gone on together since the world began, and it is still a conflict even on this plane. It is for the wise ones of earth to recognize the truth in the teaching from here, and to discard that which is not true. Learn to discriminate. Learn to discover the spirit beneath the words, and judge of its sincerity by its spiritual value."

2

COMMUNICATION

~

ONE of the arguments used against spirit communication is: "It cannot possibly be true, because so many have lost loved ones and have longed with unutterable longing for some word or sign from them; yet none has come." Such critics do not understand that there must be a receiver *here* as well as a sender there. They do not realize that the so-called sixth sense is not a universal attribute. Yet it is that uncomprehended sense that renders one capable of receiving messages that otherwise would fall on empty air. Some possess this psychic power naturally; others may partially acquire it through practice. But in both cases certain conditions are necessary for the receiving of the subtle, soundless words that cross the unseen boundary.

Speaking of the development of this psychic sense, we are told:

"You can train the mind to stop thinking. Shut out all the world and all the busy vibrations of the brain. Study passivity; practice the passive condition until you feel yourself in tune with the higher vibrations. Try to realize yourself as spirit—not bound by the limitations of the flesh—but spirit on its way to immortal life. Then, when the message comes, listen spiritually; think of yourself only as a medium through which the words may filter to your mortal mind.

For we must influence that mind, or you could not recommunicate our ideas to the world."

A former teacher of psychology told us through the pencil:

"I tried to analyze the mind processes when on earth, and found that when I could attain the most absolute silence of the brain, the most absolute passivity, I received a gleam of thought from here. I did not recognize the source then, but called it the action of the subconscious intelligence. But now I know that into that silence of the brain, thoughts and words were impressed from here. Cultivate, then, this habit of silence. Spend some portion of each day in as perfect passivity as you can attain; and wait for the inner vision, the heavenly direction, which will surely follow, if you educate your mind to receive, instead of giving out its own thought."

At another time, with a message partly written, a sentence was suddenly broken off and this followed:

"Will you stop thinking out our problem? We are trying to use your mind but it is not passive enough. It sidetracks our thought before we can impress it upon your brain. Just now we wished one thing and you thought another, and the ideas antagonized each other.

"We wish you to be so spiritually minded that we can come to you at any time, but the conditions are often contradictory. Sometimes you are passive when not psychic, and sometimes psychic when not passive."

'Which is better then, psychic power or passivity?'

"We can come through passivity more easily than through the psychic condition alone. To give up one's personality and let us take its place is true passivity, and sometimes that is lacking when the spirit is most desirous to receive."

There are many ways in which the discarnate intelligence tries to communicate with mortals. Raps, table tipping, trance speech and writing, the Ouija board, automatic writing, letters of fire—all have had their place. For ourselves the much ridiculed Ouija board brought messages both interesting and evidential, although automatic writing soon superseded the little triangle as quicker and more convenient.

"Many people begin with Ouija," we were told, "and then discover other and better ways."

We asked through what power the Ouija-board messages were sent.

"We influence your mind. If your brain does not respond, we cannot write. What we do is to impress the idea and let your brain form the words. Occasionally we can communicate our own words, but not always."

We asked about Hyslop's pictograph theory.

"It explains many things. We try to form pictures in your mind of the things we wish you to know, and the choice of the words generally comes from your own consciousness. *But the idea is ours.* Do not forget that. The words used are often not the ones we wish, but we have to take the ones called up in your brain by the idea sent across."

'It is claimed by some that the subjective mind, the subliminal mind, the latent memory, will account for the communications?'

"Some things do come from one's own mind, but only such things as have been previously put into it."

'What is the subconscious mind?'

"The subconscious is the soul, and has the attributes of the soul. Inspiration, knowledge quickly acquired, sensitiveness to impressions—all these belong to the immortal part of life."

'We were told once that conscious and subconscious minds might be better called the material and the spiritual?'

"That is true. Your spiritual body is as much with you now as it will be here: only here your spiritual impressions will not be obscured by the material senses."

'The subconscious mind plays so many tricks, many are inclined to think it might do everything that is claimed as spirit manifestation?'

"The subconscious mind is a puzzle here as well as there. But we know that beyond its curious powers of memory, there is a great field for the true spirit life. And we here can discriminate and see the difference between the action of that subconsciousness and the outpouring of words, sentences, messages, and inspirations from here. We see and know. You do not see, and hardly know. Why not trust us to separate the two activities? Your mind does get in occasionally; but we tell you so, and stop your writing. Can you not trust us to guide you?"

Sis frequently notices that remarks from that side apply closely to thoughts that are in her mind, and she has wondered if her subjective mind had influenced the pencil. One night the pencil wrote:

"We know your thought and will prove it otherwise. We are here, and we are not your mind nor your subjective self. *Answer me!* Does your subjective mind move your arm or turn your hand around like this? *Tell me!*"

During this writing her hand was twisted and turned nearly over, still keeping the pencil on the paper.

"The inner mind is a problem we have to deal with, and we are glad you are watching it too. It was to show that it was not your own mind, that so many persons on this side have come to you in peculiar ways, and have impressed you with the reality of their presence."

'You have many times told me that my own thought was getting in and preventing your expression?'

"The unintentional coloring of the messages, the tendencies of individual thought, all have their part in changing, even ever so little, the messages sent from here. It is only through the most conscientious endeavor on *both sides* that truth can filter through. The world needs to know that there is no open highway between the two worlds—between the seen and the unseen! We follow hidden trails; sometimes we break new paths; occasionally we wander far in search of an opening; and we are glad when we find any narrow way by which we may come. Yet the world scoffs if we lose a step here and there and fail of perfect knowledge."

'Can you tell us some of the difficulties from your side?'

"I think you do not comprehend the difference in the intelligence of spirits, for some have only the conception of spirit life that was theirs when they left the earth. Many are like children and could not intelligently describe the life here. Others tell things that are not true, sometimes in ignorance, sometimes in mischief. Sometimes the newly arrived spirit may still be impressed by its own earth conceptions, and may send those mistaken views to earth.

"You must not forget that upon this plane that is nearest to earth, both good and evil forces meet. All come here; and even the malicious ones can communicate with those on earth who will receive their messages. This is one of the evils of the 'open door,' and must be carefully guarded against. Do not harbor thoughts of hatred or revenge; for they will call towards you the evil-minded here, and evil is the result. Be true to high ideals."

"Be critical, but be patient and fair-minded. Cast out everything that proves to be a mistake, but keep your faith in us nevertheless. Try to see the persistent effort we are making to draw you toward us; and if we sometimes fail, try to be patient with our failures and let us try again. You must understand that the psychic power here is as necessary for communication as it is there. Not all here have that gift. We do not have it in full degree, and you say of yourself that you are not strong in psychic power; so you may understand that we are not perfect senders and you are not a perfect receiver. But if you are patient and conscientious we may get much truth to you."

A prominent teacher told us through the pencil: "The physical body is the greatest obstacle on earth in an attempt to fix the mind on spiritual things. I felt it so when there. The material senses are strong; and are intentionally so, to aid us in our earthly existence. Nevertheless it is nearly a prohibitive proposition when the mortal tries to come into communication with spirit."

"If you could only see our difficulties, you would be more patient with misunderstandings. We are of different condition and different expression, yet we try to give the marvels of this life in ways that you can understand. Be patient with our efforts to describe the indescribable."

'Can all spirits hear our voices when we speak?'

"Not all. That power is acquired by study. This circle has made it a special study and all here listen and hear your voice when you speak."

Many times our teachers there find fault with Sis's critical or doubting attitude, but once this was written:

"When we see the things that go across from here through the too credulous mediums we are glad of your skepticism. None of us wish a too uncritical attitude. There are two sources of evidence of the genuineness of our messages: one, the tests that have already been given you; the other, the messages themselves. These are definite statements, and in accord with high, spiritual life."

Quite frequently in the earlier months Sis's mind was so filled with doubt as to prove an obstacle in receiving, and the following comments were made at different times regarding it:

"Try and keep in mind all the fine and true messages that have come, and blot from your memory the mistakes that have been made. When you come here you will see our difficulties of communication, and will only wonder that anything can get through perfectly.

"You are much too doubtful, and hinder those who try to help. Yet doubt is better than too much credulity. That is why we are trying to give you proofs: that you may as honestly believe as you honestly doubt.

"Doubt is the only barrier, and you must recognize this, so that you will not lock us out.

"It is right to prove all things, but you destroy the proof by too much doubt. We are giving you things beyond the power of the senses to reveal. Your inner spirit bears testimony to the truth. Listen to that, and believe."

The dangers of false teaching from that side were called to our attention and summed up as follows:

"First, those newly arrived, with only their earth desires and knowledge. Second, the really wicked ones who have not left their malicious influences in the grave, and will lead others astray if possible. Third, those who, though good, are mistakenly so, and still cling to the convictions of their earthly education—its mistaken beliefs, creeds, etc. Those who wish to receive the truth from this side must cultivate discrimination, must desire the spiritual teaching, with its pure and unselfish conditions. Yet even then, care and always care should be taken, that the message does not suffer in transmission, and does not get entangled in the mind-thought of the medium."

Sis spoke of some wonderful spirit manifestations of which she had read, and the pencil wrote:

"You must not be disappointed because your power is of different quality. Have I not told you that the psychic gift manifests itself differently in different people? You are not a picture painter, nor a psychic letter-writer, nor have you any gift in materialization or trumpet speaking. These gifts are distributed among various people, and apparently all are necessary to influence different qualities of mind."

Clairvoyance and telepathy have been advanced many times in attempts to explain away the spirit origin of communications. To get a better understanding of what these words mean we have asked Mary about them.

'Does clairvoyance belong to the spiritual or the material part of man?'

"It is a spiritual gift entirely. It is the spirit vision and is unlimited in range. How otherwise could we go to you when you are in strange places?"

'What is telepathy?'

"It is the power to reproduce in another brain or another spirit, one's own thought. That is the shortest definition; but the power used, or the 'how' of it, would require a longer explanation. Will you wait until we can call someone who can explain more fully?"

Then after a moment or two:

"A teacher is here who says that the action of the mind is twofold— the outgoing and the incoming. The outgoing action may be—"

The pencil stopped for some time. Then another attempt was made:

"The brain receives impressions through all the material senses. But beyond these are the unexplained operations of other perceptions. These come from spirit forces—"

Then came an exceptionally long wait—so long that I finally asked if it was because Sis was lacking in psychic power.

"Not altogether. We are trying to give, in language sufficiently plain, the delicate operations of human thought—the intricate actions of brain and spirit.

"It is true that the human brain can send out thought which may find a receptive brain upon which it may be impressed. It is also true that spirit forces may carry messages from spirit to spirit. But in this latter case both sender and receiver must be sensitized by spirit perception."

'Is it through telepathy that you get messages to us?'

11

"Of course. How else could we reach you?"

'Could a mind on this plane pick out a fact from the storehouse of another's memory?'

"It would have to be an active thought in that other mind, a positive impression at the time."

Sis asked how they impressed a thought on her mind.

"You have to read our minds in a way, through our help at least, before you can express outwardly through the pencil."

I asked: 'Do you impress her mind with the thought, or does she read your mind?'

"Mary thinks it is a blending of the two influences: our desire to impress and her desire to receive. When both influences are strong, the writing goes easily."

'I suppose these efforts to impress and to receive are really some form of vibratory force?'

"Vibration is a universal power with so many expressions they are hard to define sometimes."

'I wonder if each brain is a center of power, a creator of vibrations?'

"That may be true in a way; but there are so many variations of power, that the influences would be hard to classify. Mary wishes she were more scientific; but as yet she can deal only with results, seldom with causes. The study of causes is usually for far higher planes than ours. Some are intuitional here and seem to discern knowledge far beyond. But I am not of this class, I grieve to say. In the last analysis, of course, the great Creator of all is the source of all power and all uses of it."

'Mary, I wonder if you understand that statement any better than we do?'

"Not much. We believe more than you do, but the definite knowledge is ages in advance of our present learning."

I had been reading aloud one evening an article, in which apparently the foundation question was not, "Can the dead speak to us?" but "What good will it do if they can?" And we turned to Mary for her viewpoint. Very emphatically the words were written:

"*What good?* Where are her thoughts, her knowledge of the subject? She seems wholly ignorant of the higher teachings of this life; of the happiness it has brought to anxiety; of the peace that has lightened pain; of the joy that has overcome sorrow; of the happy anticipation of this life instead of the old, terrified forebodings."

One evening Sis asked what she should write to a friend concerning certain problems she had expressed, and was met with:

"I am not your brain. Think it out yourself. You can answer if you choose. Go to it!"

We laughed at the slang, and asked if it was their thought.

"That was a reflection from earth, but it means a good deal."

I asked if the expression was in Sis's mind. Mary replied:

"We got the expression from her brain, and sent it back through her brain. We have to depend largely upon your word language to express our thought."

I asked:

'Do you ever supply your words entirely?'

"Sometimes, and occasionally use expressions quite independent of her thought; but more often impress the idea and let her choose the words."

The riddle of the subconscious mind, its action, its limitations— all have suggested many questions. One evening I said:

'We have read that this subconscious mind that you say is the soul, has no power of reasoning; it just records all knowledge received. If it has no greater power, how does it become a reasoning intelligence there?'

"The subconscious self has added powers here. Its function on earth is to deepen impressions on the brain, nerves, or ganglia; and it often reacts by suggesting those impressions again to the outer thought in very persistent ways. But, once freed from its earthly limitations, it becomes a complete personality, with all the independent thought and action of the brain, and only suggests the former life through memory."

Prof. William James gave us the following regarding the subconscious mind:

"I worked on the problem during my life on earth and found it too great for me, as the two phases interlocked so confusingly. The whole subject is, of course, clarified to me now; but the argument from here might not appeal to students there. But I will state the proposition as I now see it.

"There is an underlying consciousness in the human organism peculiarly susceptible from the outside. Dreams, visions, and germs of genius are hidden here. But this is not all. This same underlying consciousness is susceptible to the influence of spirit life and spirit intelligence; it receives messages from the discarnate as well as from incarnate influences. How to separate the spirit from the mortal influences—to discern the origin of influences playing upon this sensitive unseen part of the human organism—is the work of the intellect, that God-given power to separate, analyze, discard, or keep."

The name of Professor William James occurs at intervals throughout this book. The manner in which we made his acquaintance through the pencil is fully described in Chapter 29. In addition to this episode other valued testimony has been given confirming the reality of his presence, which testimony for various reasons has not been included in the record. For a long time after he had apparently made known his identity, Sis resisted the movement of the pencil whenever it appeared to be trying to write his name. One evening when she had several times taken her hand away from the paper at such attempts, the pencil finally wrote very forcibly:

"Will you let me come, or not? W. James."

'Do you not know why I have resisted the tendency to write your name?'

"No, I do not. Why?"

'Because I believed that one with your scholarly attainments would scarcely come to an unknown and inexperienced psychic, and I feared that my own mind was unconsciously trying to dictate the name.'

The reply came quickly:

"Remember that I was a student there of the subject you are now studying. No one can boast of knowledge here. The little we know sinks into insignificance in comparison with the great yet-to-be-known. Can you understand? We are all students. Let us learn together if together we can help."

3

TESTS AND
EVIDENTIAL MATTER

~

I AM aware that the Society for Psychical Research has devoted its energies to proving the one fact of future existence, the continuity of human life after that which we call death. The circle with which we have been in communication regard that fact as already proved, and devote their messages largely to spiritual teachings and to descriptions of spirit life. In this volume, therefore, instruction concerning future existence is of chief importance. The tests or evidential incidents which we have received have mostly been given as a stimulus to our own faith, and by way of credentials, that through them others might believe the more serious communications.

A few of these incidents are given in this chapter, trusting that they may serve to inspire belief in the messages that follow. The closing chapter of the book also contains some evidential matter.

In 1918 Margaret Cameron's book, *The Seven Purposes*, was published. Having seen it advertised, I sent for a copy. Of the contents of the book, we knew absolutely nothing; and because of this ignorance, it occurred to us to try and secure some test through its pages. We therefore asked our instructor to give us some word or sentence used in the book. After a little time this reply came:

"The name of Napoleon occurs in the book."

When the book arrived, I looked eagerly through its pages for the wished-for proof, but found only a reference to Napoleonic wars. We asked if that was what was meant, but were told:

"No; Napoleon is mentioned."

The next day Sis went through it very carefully, finding at last near its close the name Napoleon in an inconspicuous sentence of four words. This name, occurring as it does but once in the entire book, seems to us perfect evidence, for it does not seem possible that human telepathy, 'cosmic consciousness,' or other explanation can account for that one solitary word, among sixty or seventy thousand other words, being selected and impressed upon her mind to be reproduced in writing.

Before getting the book, we had been reading others in which the subject of each chapter was indicated in the headlines above the chapter. This had suggested another test from "The Seven Purposes," and we asked if they could give the title of chapter four.

"No," was the reply, "the chapter has no title."

This we also found to be correct.

The Society for Psychical Research has insisted that it is the unimportant things or occurrences that are most evidential; important objects or events being more likely to lodge in some human brain, thus bringing telepathy in as a possible explanation. We had one test of this kind, quite inconspicuous in character, but very evidential.

Several years before Dee left us her mother had passed away, and to Dee was left the final disposal of her belongings. Some of these she gave away, keeping many of the smaller things, packing these away in trunks or closets. One evening we asked Dee if she could tell us something we did not know. We had asked this before, but it had always transpired that either Sis or I had some slight knowledge or memory that spoiled the test. As an instance she wrote once:

"I am sure F. R. does not remember the curious little fork which I bought in New Orleans."

But I did remember it, and the interesting shop from which it came. But this evening she surprised us by saying:

"Mother's hatpin in lower drawer of mahogany bureau."

Now it happened that the bureau of solid mahogany which had been in her own room Dee had left in her will to a brother. It had several drawers, and underneath them all, a secret drawer. We believed naturally that the hatpin, of which we knew nothing, must have been in this drawer and had been overlooked when the bureau was taken away. So we gave up the matter as one incapable of proof. Some months later Sis and I were looking for an old, embroidered cape that had belonged to Dee's mother, and we searched through the drawers of a bureau in the room arranged for her mother, but afterward rarely used. The articles had never been looked over or touched since Dee had put them away. In the search we found in the lower drawer, underneath many other articles, this hatpin which had belonged to her mother. The bureau, though of mahogany, or at least of mahogany finish, was of much less importance than the first one, and it had not entered our minds to look in it for the hatpin. But the information given—"Mother's hatpin in lower drawer of mahogany bureau"—was literally correct. Although this may seem a trivial matter, the fact that we had no knowledge of the article— no person on earth even knew of its existence, and that the things had never been examined since they were placed there—these lift the inconsequential occurrence into a test of importance, and point to some supernormal intelligence as the source of the information.

When selecting this incident for the book we asked Dee if she had seen the hatpin in the drawer. She said she had not. She had been searching her memory for tests for us and had finally recalled placing this hatpin in the place mentioned.

One evening we were questioning concerning the residence of a person whose address we did not know. We were told:

"The address is V Street in the town of B."

We said that the street was unknown to us.

"V Street lies between B and C streets."

We were curious enough to motor to this town where we found in a new part recently laid out, that we had never seen, a short street called V lying for two blocks between B and C streets. For various reasons we did not attempt to ascertain if the person lived on this street.

The movement of Sis's arm and hand in writing are to us an evidence of a force quite unknown and quite independent of herself. Her hand rests upon the table with the pencil held loosely between the fingers. After some minutes of waiting—immediately at times— there are various little twitching movements of the fingers. Then she describes a warmth that creeps up the center of her wrist and arm. Soon afterward her hand is turned quickly back and forth on the table, a dozen times or more, and then moved to the top of the page, and the pencil begins to form the letters. This is Mary's way of announcing herself, the first word usually being her name.

When Dee comes, Sis's hand is whirled around in circles on the table many times before beginning to write her name.

Occasionally when something very emphatic is to be written, or when her own doubt gets in the way, her hand and arm to the elbow are jerked back to the shoulder with such force that frequently she involuntarily exclaims because of the pain. She has tried to reproduce this last motion voluntarily, but has never succeeded in perfectly imitating it. Sometimes when writing Sis is a little incredulous over the information given and probably resists somewhat the movement of the pencil. Then suddenly her hand will be pressed downward with much force, occasionally breaking the point of the pencil.

Mary and Dee seem to have charge of the writing, and usually are the amanuenses for others who are allowed to communicate, but who are not able to write. Occasionally, however, someone from another circle appears who has the ability to control her hand, and comes in some unusual way. She describes as follows the way that one of them came:

"My hand was resting on the table as usual, when suddenly it was raised with energy, the pencil falling from my fingers. My hand then raced back and forth across the table, the fingers unmistakably imitating piano playing. I was startled and asked:

'Who is this?'

I picked up the pencil and it wrote:

"I will not tell you."

Still more startled, I said:

'I will not write unless you tell me who you are.'

"I wish you to tell me who I am."

'I haven't the slightest idea.'

"I was in S once and saw you at your home."

'Well, that does not help me to recognize you.'

"I was stopping at E hotel."

With this there flashed into my brain the memory of a Boston friend who one summer had been at this hotel and who was very fond of piano music. I had often played for him.

'Are you W S?'

"Yes, now you have it."

Then followed a conversation which identified him quite perfectly.

At another time an acquaintance tried for three evenings before getting Sis to recognize him. Mary, who was writing, persistently withheld the name, that it might become another proof that Sis's own brain was not dictating the words. Indeed this has been a frequent method of introducing old and half-forgotten acquaintances, Mary believing that these surprises are another evidence of their presence.

Last summer while on a vacation trip, a friend asked Sis if she could possibly get news of a young soldier boy, whose home was in the same town, and who was a comrade friend of her daughter Elsie. He had been killed by a shell shortly after entering the war. She gave his name, W B, and that was all that Sis knew of him. Always doubtful of her own power, Sis had little faith that the soldier could be found; or, if so, that she could get any satisfactory message; and it was several months before she even made the attempt. Finally one evening she asked if it would be possible, in the multitude of soldiers over there, to find this one.

Mary replied:

"We are not very good in this line of work—detective work of spirit land, you might call it—but we are willing to try if you will tell us more about him."

Sis gave his name and address, and after a few moments of waiting, there was written:

"A young soldier has answered the call and says he is the one. Will you let him tell his own story? I will write for him. He says:"

"Yes, I was blown out of life there without my knowledge. The last thing I remember was starting on the rush across 'no man's land.' That is all. Then I found myself here, very confused, very doubtful even of my own identity; for thought was not clear at first. The shock to the physical had some influence, I suppose, on the spiritual part of me. But this did not last long, and I began to see other boys coming over, some frightened, some smiling and glad, some with the brave soldier air still with them. Some of them I knew, and I tried to talk to them, but they were scarcely conscious enough of the change to find words. Then we were beckoned away to some place where we found other soldier boys, who had been here longer, and had 'found themselves,' so to speak.

Then we wanted to know how the battles were going, and we were allowed to watch, and sometimes to help the boys: sometimes by sending courage to their soul thoughts; or, when wounded, to send peace thoughts, and glad thoughts even, to those who were coming over.

"The life here is all so wonderful that I can have no regret. But I wish I could send word to my parents. I want them to know that I live, and live far more perfectly than before. And I am glad to be here, only I do not want them to grieve."

'Can you tell me how you look?'

"I have been trying to impress my presence upon your mind. I can say, slender of body, straight, and not too tall, with blue eyes— or dark eyes of some kind,—hanged if I know their color!"

"But anyway, tell Elsie I am the same boy she used to know, and I want her to think of me with pleasure, believing my life here is larger and better than I could ever have made it there. Good bye. W B."

'That sounded all right, Mary. Do you think he is the right one?'

"Yes. He is a bright boy, and we think he told the exact truth; but we did not know his earth life, and could not prove his identity except through his words."

Sis wished he had given more proof that he really was W B. Almost immediately the pencil wrote:

"Try to be passive and take this as he tells it, for he returned as you talked of him."

Then evidently to convince her of his identity, he said:

"I went to a dance with Elsie not long before I went away. We joked each other about the new dances and she tried to teach me the new steps, and I only stepped on her toes a few times! Perhaps she will remember. I was not in the home town when I enlisted. I enlisted in another city."

After a time Sis sent this account to her friend, and in reply was told that W B had enlisted not in his home town, but in another; that he returned to his home for a few days before his regiment left, and during that time took Elsie to a dance; and that afterward, when he said goodbye to Elsie's mother, he laughingly told her that he "couldn't dance, could only step on Elsie's toes."

Three strongly evidential circumstances occur here: that he had not enlisted in his home town; that he had taken Elsie to a dance; and that the joke about stepping on Elsie's toes was repeated from 'over there.' Another case in which the small things of life prove big in an evidential manner.

Mr. Edwin Friend, who lost his life on the ill-fated *Lusitania*, was at one time, I understand, connected with the American Society for Psychical Research. Mr. J of this city had been intimately acquainted with Friend, and came one evening to see if we could get any communication from him. Sis took up the pencil, and after a short wait, it wrote:

"Dee is here. What can we do for you?"

We explained that Mr. J would like to talk to his former acquaintance, Edwin Friend.

"Wait a little. We are sending a messenger for him." Soon the writing commenced again with:

"He is here and is glad to know that his old-time friend is present, and says if he thought J would respond, he would shake hands with him."

21

Mr. J said later that to meet him with a joke was quite characteristic. Then Mr. Friend asked if Mr. J remembered their talks together, and that J was not as doubtful of a future life as he himself had been. Recalling their former conversations, Mr. J admitted this was true. Mr. Friend continued:

"He was something of an investigator, but not along the same lines as myself."

This was also true, and entirely unknown to us.

Then almost immediately Professor William James took the pencil and wrote these sentences:

"Friend is better looking than when on earth. His teeth are perfect. His eyes do not need glasses."

This was a complete puzzle to Sis as she had never known anything about Friend. But to Mr. J they suddenly assumed a particularly evidential character. Mr. Friend, he said, was a very homely man, and was quite conscious of his appearance. His teeth, it seems, were so prominent as to be disfiguring. And owing to trouble with his eyes, he wore glasses. So that the three sentences in regard to personal appearance took on the importance of tests.

Then Mr. J asked if Edwin Friend, as a test, could tell him now what theory it was that he had advanced in a letter to a mutual friend. Mary asked twice to have the question repeated. Then there was a short wait, after which Mary wrote:

"Edwin Friend was trying to remember the theory in question. The open truth here, the perfection of knowledge, make us forget sometimes our halting beliefs over there."

Finally Mr. Friend wrote:

"I was absorbed in the telepathy theory to an extent, and that telepathy plays a great part in communication between the two worlds."

This, Mr. J said, was the subject of the letter.

He then spoke of having a photograph of Mr. Friend, and the pencil wrote:

"Well, he is welcome to it! Tell him he had better hide it under a curtain though."

Sis remarked that he had not lost his sense of fun over there. He replied:

"We have lots of it, and James and I are constantly joking each other. I get after his pink pajamas, and he calls me a stage beauty."

It was some time before Mr. J realized the relevancy of this last. But suddenly he saw in it another test, as Edwin Friend had been very fond of private theatricals, and often took feminine parts in some comedy, thus becoming the "stage beauty" of the play. The "pink pajama" incident is familiar to anyone who has read the books by Prof. Hyslop, the late secretary of the American Society for Psychical Research.

At the last minute before the final arrangement of this book, Mary put through another test. It is best given as a copy from our records, as follows:

July 15th. Mary has been working for a week on a test that had been arranged in their circle. It began on the 9th, when she said:

"Try and be patient with our effort to send you messages. What we wish now is not easy to get across, and so we wish your patient effort. Will you try now or wait until another time?"

'I will try now if you think I am psychic enough.'

"We wish to tell you of a new idea that one of the circle has suggested. It is that you—The circle wish you to try to—"

"Mary says she will wait. You do not take my thought tonight. Mary will keep the thought for another time."

Then on the 12th, she wrote:

"We wish to give you a few words if you can take them. We here are planning some—"

"Will you try to keep passive until I can get through our thought. We wish to try to give you a word or two that may connect in a sentence some other evening as a sort of test.

"Try first a word meaning patience."

'Will the word endurance do?'

"Yes, that will do. Write it down."

'Endurance.'

"Yes, that will do. Then think of a word meaning—"

The pencil failed to make anything but illegible marks.

'Are you trying to write the word love?'

"Yes."

'Love!'

"That is all for this time. Mary says: Keep those two words separate from other writing and let us add others."

'Do you wish some other word than love?'

"No, that is right. Keep those two words apart. We know that you have no idea of what is coming, therefore your mind is not doing this."

(On two other evenings Mary continued these endeavors to get certain words across. There was much difficulty with two of them; so, for the sake of brevity, several pages of the record are omitted, but the method was the same as has been shown.)

This afternoon Mary asked Sis to write down the words received: *Endurance, Love, Electricity, Society, Thought.* Almost before the last letter was written Mary continued rapidly with the following:

"*Endurance* is the thought of many on that plane when they should strive to make *love* the first in power and achievement; for love is the *electric* thrill that can mold society into spiritual *thought.*

"That is the idea. Now phrase it differently."

Tonight the following was written:

"We are all here, all the circle, and all are rejoicing that the test went through fairly well. What do you think of it?"

Sis said she had not rewritten it yet.

"The wording can be changed, and the words themselves, if you think of a better synonym. Mary thinks of it more as a test, but the sentiment is what we all believe too."

I said I thought it an excellent test, but feared it would be criticized because both words and sentences came through Sis's pencil.

"Will you be patient even with critics. They are clearing the subject of much that is false. We have one with us who is always a balance to us in this respect, William James, for he insists on the value of tests and of criticism. He thinks this is a good test because you were so doubtful and took the words so slowly. And at the last I wrote the sentence too quickly for your mind to even begin to form a sentence."

'The words seemed so incongruous, I was wondering how it was possible to include them in a sentence.'

"Yes. I feared your mind might unconsciously suggest a sentence, therefore I wrote hastily what we had decided upon. But we had not put it into the earthly expression, and in the haste the phrasing was rather crude."

This style of test was so easy for them to arrange that Mary has given several of them, "skeleton sentences," as she calls them; suggesting words through the pencil that apparently had no possible connection, and then dashing off complete and rational phrases including these words.

Two of these are given below.

One afternoon Sis took the pencil to ask Mary a question. But Mary had other wishes, it seemed, for she wrote at once:

"Mary wishes that you try to give us a time of passivity, that we may try some experiment in—"

'In thought reading?'

"Yes."

'Now?'

"Yes, now."

"The word we wish is used to denote a play."

Sis offered several words, but Mary said:

"No, play is the word we wish. Put it down."

Later, Mary used the word drama instead.

"Now try a word meaning—."

Sis mentioned some word.

"Not that, but another meaning the same."

'Space?'

"Space will do. Now try a word for the—"

'Higher?'

"Not higher, but the same meaning."

'Upper?'

"Yes, upper. The last word must be one meaning action."

'Motion?'

"Try another of that meaning."

'Movement?'

"No, but nearly."

'Progress?'

"Yes. Now write them together. I have to work through your mind."

'Play, Space, Upper. Progress.'

Then, as before, Mary wrote rapidly:

"The *drama* of life began in space;

It moved to *upper* and higher things;

And in all the life of unknown worlds

'Tis progress that is the soul of things."

Then again, after similar preliminary writing and guessing, the following words were written:

'Existence. Life. Stillness. Heavenly.'

And immediately Mary dashed off the following sentences containing these words:

"A *heavenly stillness* comes to the soul

And drives away all jarring strife.

'Tis then that *existence* is reaching its goal,

For then it comes near to the heavenly *life*."

Aside from all the actual tests here given, there are incidents in connection with the writing itself that have furnished an accumulation of evidence showing the presence of a reasoning personality, only explainable as a discarnate mind, or rather, many of them.

First, is the plainly marked difference in many of the communications, one from another. The messages and remarks from Dee are often characteristic of her personality, as known so well in life by Sis and myself. Those from Mary frequently show evidences of certain traits that are not manifested by any other communicator.

Halevans' apparent impatience and his style were entirely distinct from anyone else. While the writings signed "W. James" may not show any great resemblance to his published books and letters, yet there is a recognizable similarity of construction and continuity of thought common to most of them, though given on different dates.

There is no reasonable way of explaining the many different persons who have appeared and communicated, except by admitting that they are what they pretend to be, unless one claims multiple personality of the subconscious mind of the receiver or medium. As this would require the personality to be split up into more than a hundred parts, each apparently quite complete in itself, such an explanation fails to explain much.

Then how can the skeptic explain the following incidents and many similar ones?

When Mary was telling of the inhabitants of one of the planets, the pencil suddenly stopped. After a short pause she resumed the writing with this remark:

"I was asking if I might describe how they walked."

Unless it was the subconscious mind of the receiver, or a portion of it, doing the writing, who would it be, who could it be, except a discarnate spirit? And pray explain why the medium's subconscious mind, if attempting to palm itself off as someone else, should suddenly feel it necessary to ask permission to make some statement. Such an explanation would only complicate the situation.

Many times when some certain person is called for, the reply will be, "Wait a little, I will call him;" and after a few moments the person called will appear. Several times after such a pause the reply was: "He cannot come just at present;" or "He is far away just now."

Dee and Mary are almost invariably present, yet two or three times when Dee was wanted, Mary has replied, "Dee is with her class of children."

We were much surprised once to find Dee and Mary both absent, and other members of the circle did the writing. To add to the surprise, an old friend of Sis made himself known after several attempts—a person whom Sis had not even thought of in years. During the writing Dee and Mary suddenly arrived, saying they had been on a long trip to another planet; and Mary wrote:

"Mary is here, and fine things have been going on without me! But I guess I will have to forgive you, for the test was pretty good after all. I was watching the last part of it and think you were rather surprised at the outcome."

Can you possibly conjure up any explanation of, or even any reason for, such remarks, except a spiritistic one?

Then, the many personalities that have been introduced, and the manner of their introduction, all have been interesting. Mary and Dee both say this is done principally to furnish evidence in various ways. Some of these persons introduced have been recognized with great difficulty. One never has been able to bring himself to Sis's memory. One of these persons wrote a strong plea for earth people to study more concerning the future life, and promised to give another message next evening.

So, the next evening we were expecting this, and Mary said it would be given. A little hesitancy was shown in beginning the writing, and after a paragraph had come, it was discovered that someone else entirely was writing. Later, Mary explained that this second person had come to them just when they were ready to write, and the first person had given way for the second.

Is not the logical and sensible explanation of these surprises that of actual spirit communication?

There is plainly evident a strong desire to have as much of the world as possible receive information concerning the future life. In trying to give this, there is found considerable difficulty in getting the medium to write it as wished. Formal messages are tried and abandoned.

Many new persons are introduced so that in telling their stories, information can be gotten through. Even this method is not entirely satisfactory, so bits of information are passed out in ordinary conversation. All sorts of schemes are resorted to in attempts to overcome the doubts and caution and other inhibitions of the receiver.

The information received, the manner in which it is put through, the evident purpose for which it is sent, the arguments used and the explanations given—all show a reasoning intelligence working logically toward an end or purpose. And this purpose is to call the attention of earth people to better paths leading to the future life.

4

THE AWAKENING

~

S OME of us have watched by the bedside of one whom we loved, in that last mysterious moment when life has separated from the body, leaving it to return to the elements from which it came. And this life? We have questioned: Where does it go, and how—this life, soul, spirit, this indestructible, yet invisible something? How does it begin the strange unaccustomed existence, of which we have known so little? These are the questions we have asked again and again, and the replies have given us much to think about.

"The awakening," we are told, "is a gradual coming into consciousness; yet this unconscious condition differs in different people. A case of long suffering, or brain trouble, or extreme ignorance, or even materialism, might result in a long sleep or dream condition. But the unconscious soul is even then beginning its education for the new life, through the suggestions given by watchful guides and teachers.

"There is a great difference in the length of time of this unconscious period of the discarnate soul. Soldiers killed in battle often become conscious almost immediately. They go out in vigorous health; the life principle has not been disturbed by sickness or age. A very great influence abides in the habit of thought while on earth, whether it is a spiritual conviction or a material belief. Many times the spirit comes over into the dream state with beliefs that have been deeply impressed upon it by mortal conditions. For instance, one who had suffered years of extreme illness and pain, remained many weeks in the belief that she was still in her poor suffering body. She complained of the cold; called the nurse to cover her up; and could not understand why the attendant was not more watchful, and why her children could not come to her."

"Many undeveloped souls are constantly coming. We meet and care for them and lead them patiently onward into better knowledge. To meet those who have tried to do right on earth, even though mistaken in their beliefs, is a work of love here, and the way is made bright for them by the friendliness of their reception.

"There are circles whose principal work is to care for those who arrive without any conception of this life—ignorance pure and simple; people who have never thought or questioned beyond the earthly existence.

"Many come with their mortal habits of selfishness, pride, ignorance, and folly. These faults must be eliminated before they can begin to progress. It is our happiness to watch this growth out of selfishness into service, out of pride into humility, out of ignorance into knowledge, out of folly into wisdom. Sometimes the pathway upward is long indeed, and filled with repentance and sorrow. Yet through these they may be led into the true life of the spirit. The ones who are longest retarded, and who come into spiritual joy with almost incredible slowness, are those who have no wish to change, who are wedded to their sins, and could not be happy with pure and noble spirits. For these a lifetime—or even many lifetimes—may pass before their desires change from evil to good."

In strong and beautiful contrast with such experience is the arrival of one whom we had known during her loving and unselfish earth life. We asked what were her recollections of the awakening.

"My recollections here?" was the reply, "To me now there seems only the remembrance of light, that was so clear and beautiful. I had been for a time unconscious, resting as it seemed. Then I began to see vaguely, and to hear exquisite sounds, and I slowly came into the consciousness that I had passed over and that I still lived. Then my good angel, Mary, so surrounded me with her tenderness and affection that I could nevermore be otherwise than happy."

Later, this same "good angel, Mary," said this of our friend:

"I was sent to receive her, as I have been sent to many others. She was long in the restful state before consciousness came, and I watched and loved her from the first. I saw her soul as it came into its spiritual inheritance, and her pure spirit was so beautiful that my love was captured before she even knew me."

Another person described her passing in this way:

"I did not know I had passed into this life, and I experienced the dream condition you have heard so much about. Then I began to see 'men as trees walking,' as the Bible has it, and I wondered. But I thought it part of the attack that I was vaguely conscious of having experienced. When I finally came to a knowledge of this life, I found myself as ignorant as a child."

Another said:

"I was too ill to realize my danger, and passed over without knowing it. But, oh, my dear! I was met with such tenderness and love that my life seemed all at once transformed. And I have desired nothing so much as to grow into the same loving service for others. I am with a circle who meet many who, like me, come over alone; and the care that we may give them is a joy greater than I can describe."

5

THE SPIRIT BODY

~

IT is difficult for the human mind to realize any conditions that lie outside the five physical senses. These, since man was created, have been his guide and protection until he can scarcely conceive of intelligent life existing without them. The spirit body, which cannot be tested through these senses—sight without eyes, hearing without ears, thought without brain, touch, movement, all without the physical equipment—is nearly, if not quite, incomprehensible.

Our repeated questions have brought answers which have enlightened our dull comprehension to a certain extent. We asked one evening if the statement was true that spirit bodies were etheric.

"It is true that our bodies are etheric in substance; and we admire more and more their adaptation to spiritual environment. We do not have the material senses, or the material substance; we are constructed, so far as the body is concerned, of finer material. We are not conscious of our bodies, for they serve us without pain or weariness, and we are not constantly taking care of them as on earth."

'Can you see each other?'

"We can see each other, but perceive through different senses. You need not fear for the expression of spiritual life or spirit body, for all is far better than any you have imagined."

'You do not breathe; do you have lungs?'

"No, nor any of the other organs necessary for earth life. The material organs were created for man's use during his material life and are quite unnecessary here. We do not need eyes nor ears, for sight and hearing are through spirit powers; yet we have the semblance of these in our spirit forms. We do not need the organs of speech, nor the mouth, nor other organs of the material outfit; yet the outline of the material form is beautiful, and we can well assume that form for ourselves. We have no material limbs; yet when you see us the likeness will not be missing. We love the old familiar form and it becomes more beautiful here, and remains."

'Do you have the sense of touch?'

"We might if we chose, for spirit can give sensation as perfectly as the nerves, but we do not often require this."

One evening Mary wrote:

"Many friends are here, wishing news from earth."

'Are they all in this room?'

"We can get into smaller compass than you imagine; yet if you could see us you would recognize everyone."

'What are you, anyway? Just a thought floating around?'

"No! We have forms, and they are very like our earthly ones, only better. Spirit is not confined to any particular length, breadth, or thickness. Nevertheless, we have bodies, and do have size if we wish."

I spoke of reading of debates among monks of olden times over the question of how many angels could stand on a needle's point.

"That is a good question. I know I could balance on a needle's point, or I could occupy as much room as I ever did on earth."

'How did you come into the room? The windows and doors are closed.'

"You need not think that walls are obstacles to us. We pass through them as easily as light passes through glass."

'How does the wall appear to you?'

"Something like a cloud, through which we move as easily as you would walk through a fog."

'You are like an X-ray then?'

34

"That is a good comparison as far as movement through obstacles is concerned."

'How about rain and storms?'

"All weather is bright to us. Changes in temperature make no difference, nor clouds, nor rain. We could move away from any tornado if we chose, or we could stay in it and enjoy its motion. We could outride any tempest in a flash, and the rain cannot even moisten the texture of our raiment. Can't you understand, you human child? Wait till you come and we will prove to you how superior we are to nature's elements."

'Can you touch each other: shake hands, for instance?'

"What are those motions except to express thought? We do not need such expressions, for with us thought expresses itself without medium of touch or of speech, although we can use these if we wish."

Sis, always doubtful and confused about the powers of spirit, asked:

'With your spirit sight, can you see Dee?'

"She is here and smiling that you are still so ignorant of spirit power. She is near you and could touch you, yet you are doubtful of her presence."

'How does she look?'

"As she looked when on earth, only far more beautiful. Her robes fall about her with soft, cloud-like radiance, and express the same sense of harmony that she loved on earth."

Then Sis asked Dee to tell her how Mary looked.

"Mary has dark eyes and is taller than I am. We are not alike in looks, but are alike in perceptions, tastes, and desires. We have different work, and each has different interests; yet we are closely related. Can you understand?"

'How about her dress?'

"She wears delicate colors, as nearly all do; sometimes rose color, pink, or lavender, but in shades more delicate than any you know. We are never afraid of injuring our robes, for they are not subject to wear or soil. They are never in the way, and we do not step on or get entangled in them.

"We are clothed in garments that correspond to our mental and spiritual condition. You will appear in a simple white garment at first, and this will change as you change. Mental qualities express themselves outwardly, and different minds express different colors. Minds that are filled with doubt are sometimes clothed in incongruous colors. The destructive forces have coarse garments of the most discordant colors. They imagine themselves in gorgeous apparel. But they will sometime see themselves as they are, which will be when they reach out for something better.

"The clothes are made by thought processes, as are all our beautiful surroundings. We are clothed when we first arrive, and only the color remains for us, which is decided by our own thought lives. We can change when we choose, but few changes are made, for the material is indestructible."

We had been talking of dress one evening, and jokingly asked about the prevailing fashions there.

"We could never describe the fashions here, for they change with lightning swiftness. We would have to describe the prevailing thought instead. Thought manifests itself in changes of color. Character always differentiates the appearance. The appearance is lovely in proportion as the spirit is lovely. Dress is more than external adornment; it becomes a sort of symbol of character."

One evening my grandfather came, and Mary said:

"He is very bright and happy looking, and if you could see his perfect form and youthful appearance, you would not be calling him grandfather."

I spoke of his stooping shoulders when on earth, and Mary came back with this:

"Must I repeat, that no physical imperfection appears in the spirit form? He is not surprised that you remember his bent figure, but thinks he will be able to surprise you when you come."

A young soldier of whom we had known had been blown to atoms by a shell. We asked if that would interfere with the spirit's entrance into that life.

"The body does not imprison the spirit; neither can the spirit be injured. The soul of the young soldier would arrive here as perfectly as if borne on angel wings."

'Then spirit is not subject to accidents?'

"Spirit is superior to all conditions. I could meet lightning without sensation, or ride on the wings of a tornado, or drop into the greatest heat, or move among polar snows, and all sensations would be pleasant. Spirit is the controlling power. I do not quite know how to express it, but spirit is above and beyond any conflict of the elements, or any material conditions. In our movement through the ether, we have no sense of obstruction, and we pass easily through matter that you consider solid. We are infinitely finer than any material known on earth."

'Could you descend into the earth?'

"It is through spirit that the treasures of the earth have been found. It is through spiritual impressions on the mind of man that he has been sent to seeking and using the hidden riches which are there for the finding."

Speaking of the higher planes, we are told:

"Life on the higher planes is more ethereal than here, and all conditions are more ethereal. Coming to this plane from a higher one is a little like descending from an altitude where the air is light, to a lowland where the air is dense. Like a life accustomed to the rarefied air of mountain tops, descending into deep pits of the earth, where the air is too heavy for them to breathe."

6

SPIRIT SENSES

~

W E have been schooled by earthly teachers into the belief that once we have passed the gateway of death, the fair land of promise—the paradise, the heavenly home—would lie before us in all its perfection, and in one moment of rapture we would see and understand, and immediately all knowledge as well as vision would be ours. Instead of this instantaneous fairyland of delight, we have been told of the more normal one of growth, of steadily increasing knowledge, the continued unfolding of new fields of vision; and always beyond, the unending vistas of greater knowledge, greater marvels and greater joy.

It is said that "at first even the spiritual vision is dim, and many mistakes are made." And one speaking of his own experience said:

"I did not attain spiritual powers at once; the spiritual vision was especially long in coming. This caused an unnatural appearance of the surroundings, and as I could not discern objects distinctly, I was often mistaken. The hearing was also blurred and indistinct. But everything appeared so much better than the life I had left, that even then I was happy."

Prof. William James has written many times for us in later months. He said one evening:

"I have been trying patiently to perfect my hearing of earth sounds. This is a study, as well as most of the other gifts we strive for here. I have improved so much that I can often hear your conversation together. I can see better also, and can distinguish the different personalities of individuals there."

We asked if he could explain clairvoyance.

"Clairvoyance is the sight of the spirit; the sight which has its own light, and can penetrate distance; can visualize behind walls of stone, or even through the earthly covering of mortal bodies. For it can see mind, as I just now saw your mind, and the question poising and ready to be liberated by speech."

At another time we asked Mary if she could see us.

"We can see you and are here in the room with you."

'You are not much more material than an X-ray?'

"Not much; but we have all that is essential. Do not for a moment think that we are lacking in anything that goes to make up life, perception, or intelligence."

'But there is a limit to what you can see of material things, is there not?'

"I can hardly explain spiritual vision; but it does not depend upon the optic nerve."

'Does it depend upon someone here?'

"I think that has something to do with it; for I see you when talking to you, but not always at other times."

There is, no doubt, much misunderstanding in regard to the ability of the discarnate spirit to discern material things and material happenings. If we think of our departed friends as active entities on the other side, most of us imagine them as watching with increased interest those they have left behind. Perhaps few stop to analyze what they really do think and imagine; but usually, I think, there is a vague impression that the spirit can see everything in our daily life, and know all we are doing and even thinking. This seems to be far from the truth. A few who are strongly psychic by nature and fitted by study and training for such observation, can do this. Of the others, only those who are "linked by a strong bond of attraction" of love or sympathy have such powers. And the extent of this vision and knowledge, outside of psychic clairvoyance, is in proportion to the strength of these ties.

Even when we are seen by our loved ones, they often only see our soul or inner spirit, and frequently are unable to read a single one of our thoughts.

One evening we sat quite a long time without any manifestation from 'over there,' and we jokingly said:

'Guess they must have gone to a picture show.'

Immediately the pencil dashed off:

"You are right. We have been to a picture show."

'Just what do you mean by that?'

"We mean we can see so much that is beyond your vision that is wonderful, that we can well call it a picture show. We not only see your surroundings, but we see your spirit selves, which are far finer than your earthly ones."

These chapters were all read aloud for their correction. When we came to the above, Mary added the following:

"That is a limited answer. If you could for one instant visualize what we actually see, you would not wonder at our expression."

'Can you tell us just what you are seeing right now?'

"The working of the human mind is an increasing wonder to us here who were so blind to it all on earth. The mind occupies the first place in our vision; then the material by which it is encased; then its environment and the influences playing upon it. 'The Story of the Mind,' one might call it. In an earthly picture show, the writer of the play stumbles darkly along the same path, only more often bringing to the light the tragedies and woes which are generated in the mind. The story as we see it here is so often written in the pure white light of unselfish purpose, that we wish we could give this picture to you. Many influences are there, unseen by you, that to our sight glow with heavenly radiance, and it is the influence of such vision that keeps us from despair over the earthly mistakes and crimes."

Once we were told:

"Your spiritual body is as much with you now as it will be here; only there its powers are obscured by the five senses. Those five senses make havoc with spiritual logic and instruction. Why not give your study, thought, and investigation to what is beyond and outside of those five earthly and material powers? They are given to serve you through the earthly phase of your journey hitherward, but were not meant to chain, clog, and darken the higher impressions. Five senses! You have a hundred here, and all more perfect than any of the five."

'Are you not exaggerating in that?'

"Not a bit! Look with spirit sight, hear with spirit hearing, comprehend with spirit understanding, and the vastness of the universe, the majesty of its glory and beauty, will make you scorn the five pitiful senses."

Partly in an explanatory way, another communicator wrote:

"We have perceptions which might rank as senses. The five earthly ones are all so increased and multiplied by their varied powers, that they might well be called additional ones. Then we have perceptions not dependent upon sight, hearing, touch or taste. These belong to spirit intuitions."

'I suppose you hardly have need of the sense of taste?'

"Not as you know it. Although there are many things that appeal to us almost like that sense. We have fruits and flowers and many other things, that appeal to both taste and smell. But we do not gain them through material organs as you do."

We asked about other sensations.

"We have sensations analogous to the mortal ones, though only in a spiritual sense. We do not need to clasp the hand to show our friendship. There is no need of kisses or other expressions of affection. We have the spiritualized form of them which is higher and finer."

'Do you use language there?'

"We can speak if we wish; and oratory, poetry and lessons are given in word language. But in ordinary intercourse ideas flash from mind to mind without need of words. We speak with spirit organs, as we use other spirit powers; but this you can hardly understand as yet."

'Can you read the written words here, or do you get them through our minds?'

"I read mostly through the mind; I have not learned the other way yet. Others can read written words, but I have not progressed so far."

'If there were a picture in this room that neither of us knew or saw, could you tell what it was?'

"I doubt it, unless it was the likeness of someone I knew and loved, and I am not sure even of that. We see your soul or spirit selves, and do not discern the physical very clearly except as a shadow of the soul. It is like seeing your true self through a veil; the material flesh is the veil. A picture does not have the inner spirit. It is only an impression of a material body, and that is hard for us to see. Some can see perfectly all material things, but my own power is at present limited."

7

SPIRIT LAND

~

PERHAPS now we can picture the soul with its newly acquired powers of observation, its spiritual vision. What of its environment? What is there to see?

It is practically beyond the powers of the material brain to conceive of the reality, the substantiality, of the spirit world, the objects that the inhabitants of spirit land see with the perception that corresponds to our sight. From various descriptions that we have read, and from the information given to us, there is reason to believe that the landscapes, trees, and buildings of the spirit world are more "real," are more nearly a material substance, than we might think. The suggestion given elsewhere in the book, that mind in that realm has power to build up these objects from electrons by using laws of which we know nothing, gives us food for thought.

The results of such work are not perceptible to our senses, of course; but they are seen by the new powers of spirit. How little we would know of air and most forms of gas if our other senses registered them no better than does our sight! Can we not imagine a sight perception so superior to the one we now possess, that sensations would be registered and recognized, not only from gases, but from even more tenuous "material"? Is there reason for denying that electrons may be controlled by laws we have not known? We certainly do not deny the reality of atoms or molecules; yet what inconceivable numbers of these must be massed together before they can be sensed by any of our five material powers! Is it safe to assert the impossibility of some other combination of these, or of electrons, than those we have known? Scientists of course are loath to take any hypothesis into consideration involving unknown laws. But most of them accept ether, the characteristics of which seem in some ways to defy known laws. This means that if ether exists, it is controlled by laws as yet unrecognized. There may be other unrecognized forces. There may be "substance" and "material" in the spirit realm!

Of course our inquisitive minds were early seeking information as to what the spirit world was like. Were there trees and flowers and buildings? Were there mountains and rivers and beautiful landscapes?

"There are gardens and flowers here of exceeding beauty. They are formed by thought processes according to certain laws, and only those who love beauty and form are entrusted with the work. Architecture is also a thought product. You need not try to understand the operation, for it belongs to spirit and to spirit alone."

One who was at that time engaged in architecture and in color formation there told us one evening:

"We are building and building, making halls and rooms and houses in the most exquisite way imaginable, and never for a moment have to halt for lack of means or lack of material. Truly the 'many mansions' are here, and beautiful beyond description. When you come you will have a home that will express your most artistic fancy and your greatest desire for beauty."

'Can you give us a description of the building you use as a meeting hall?'

"I will try. It is not of marble or wood or stone, but a beautiful building of white material, shining and pure, with dome of golden color, with halls and rooms and various meeting places and appointments for the different studies."

'Do you have pictures?'

"Pictures are used to illustrate many different studies; but these are more evanescent thoughts thrown forward pictorially to illustrate something in the lesson."

'Do you have no permanent pictures?'

"Pictures are painted by artists here as they are on earth, only with different canvas and color. But once painted, they can remain until replaced by others, or until the artists themselves erase them."

'Does this hall of learning appear to each person the same in every detail?'

"The building remains; and those who enter find the same halls, the same rooms, the same laboratories, the same equipment for explanation, and the same books—if I may so name some of the thought impressions. You seem to think there is no substantiality to spirit, while we know it is the only substantiality."

Being told that they were creations of the mind, it was very difficult for us to realize their permanence, and we more than once asked about it.

'You say the park or landscape is a creation of the mind?'

"Yes; but more real than you imagine of mental pictures, because all can see and enjoy the same."

'Is this mental picture of a park a mirage or a reality?'

"It is a reality, for mind is the only reality here."

'Is such a picture permanent, or does it change?'

"It would remain until altered by command. It has permanency affected only by the directing wills of the powers who control."

'Can you tell us what the flowers are like?'

"Try to imagine a flower that neither fades nor withers, yet may disappear to make room for other flowers when so desired. We do not destroy, but they become a part of the etheric substance again, to be used later in other creations. We can produce growing plants if we choose, and watch the bud come into flower, and leaf and stem perfect themselves. Or we can create the flower full grown and beautiful."

Once when Dee had been telling us of her little pupils, and of their play in the gardens, she said:

"The gardens devoted to children are far more beautiful than any known to you. The flowers are of exquisite beauty, many-hued, and with forms unknown on earth. There are lakes with water crystal-clear; fountains softly splashing; tree-shaded nooks and corners; and wide, open places for games or play. Can you imagine children playing in lake or fountain without spoiling their beautiful garments, or catching cold? Can you imagine a sunshine that does not burn, or winds that bring no dust, or play and exercise followed by no fatigue?"

'Will we be able to see the beautiful landscapes from the first, when we arrive?'

"You will be able to enjoy nature from the first. We have landscapes here, and can go on to other scenes as we wish, the same as you travel to new scenes and places."

'Are there changes there? Do the landscapes change? Do your beautiful flowers change?'

"The things we wish to remain are stable. But our wishes change, and our surroundings adapt themselves to our thoughts. Would you like to live in an old house when a more beautiful one could be yours? Would you there keep a garden of weeds, if your larger intelligence could produce flowers? Everything here evolves as we evolve. Growth and change are the laws of life both here and there."

One evening we called for Dee, and Mary replied that she would soon arrive. When she came Sis said:

'Dee, I was thinking of your coming when I called, and wondering how you came; whether you walked on the ground or came through the air?'

"I was coming quickly, so that my feet did not exactly touch the ground; but I can walk if I choose."

'What is the ground like? Can you describe it?'

"We walk on solid ground, you might say, but not as earth ground would seem. It has no dust; no rain can make it impassable, nor mud to soil our garments or feet. It is more like a glass foundation. That is not a good comparison, but it is as near as I can think just now. Always smooth, dry, dustless; and always beautiful in its winding way or broad thoroughfare.

We may walk through groves, or by running stream, or sit by lake or fountain. Or we may meet others in the broad and beautiful streets.

Yet we do not need to use these paths or streets unless we choose, for we can come more quickly, rising above all the habitations and all the natural loveliness, and move swiftly through the air.

"Does this satisfy you? We are not confined to anyone way, but can choose our own."

'Can you in any way describe what the ground is made of?'

"Not exactly, any more than we can describe the material of which our homes are made. There are some things here that are so nearly indescribable to you, that all we can do is to make an attempt at their appearance. No spirit material is exactly like the mortal, and our names for them would convey no meaning to you."

'Do the trees and flowers there have any life that is comparable to plant life here?'

"The life of a plant here depends upon the thought of the one who conceived it. For flowers and plants are the work of artists, and each artist has a different conception of beauty. Hence, we have a variety and beauty not known on earth."

At another time she said:

"There is no beauty on earth equal to the beauty here. Never fear for lack of variety of expression, or lack of appreciation."

I said it seemed rather vague to us, because it was so difficult to think of all these things as more than unstable visions, where there was no solid material as we know material.

"You cannot understand the conditions, but you need not think of these things moving away from you, disappearing like a dream. They stay! I saw the same beautiful creations when I first came that I see now. We love our surroundings and do not change them except for some vital reason. If a tree was in your way, would you not cut it down? Or a pillar that did not correspond with the rest of the architecture, would you not replace it? Something of the kind might induce a change here, but we rest in the very permanency of the things we love.

"Nevertheless, you must not forget that the heavenly universe is limitless, and millions of spirits are creating new homes and new surroundings out in space. And the beauty grows and grows, and a 'change of scene' can be had in an instant's time by a journey into space. Spirit is the only thing that persists. Then why cannot you conceive of its permanence?"

'If you have so many vast territories, I should think it might interfere with movement to other planets and universes?'

"Not at all. Remember we are not confined to the ground. We are not hindered by obstacles, for we move over, as easily as in a straight line. Vast spaces are given to beauty of scene or of landscape, but remember the ease and quickness with which we move. What would a hundred miles be, for instance, for light to travel?"

Again when speaking of beauty, we were told:

"We have everything that pertains to beauty, either of dress or scenery or gems or anything else. Make no mistake! Your world has nothing to compare with the beauty of this!"

I had been questioning about their surroundings in various ways, and asked here:

'I realize that beautiful things are there. But I was thinking that one would not need many things there that are used on earth: such as a pocket-knife, a pencil, a sewing machine, or an automobile; and I wonder just what will be there?'

"Suppose you needed a knife, why, then create one! That is within the range of spirit power. But you would find it quicker to perform the service without the bother of making a knife. And this applies to other things as well. We do not need the sewing machine when we can create the dress by quicker and better means."

'Yes, I realize that you really need little that we have here. Even your houses are not needed for protection from storms and cold.'

"We do love our homes, and we love to have them beautiful; but they do not require the care that is given earthly homes. Beauty is care-free here. We wish we could give you a picture of our home, but you would want to come right away if we did!"

After this chapter was arranged thus far, Mary and Dee, in answer to a question, gave an account of their experiences and education there. This gives further information on the subjects mentioned in the last three chapters, and is given here just as we have it on our records, except that a portion is omitted that is of too intimate a nature to publish. Mary said:

"I was very ignorant when I came over. I was dazed at first and did not recognize myself as spirit. But my good angel was there and I was led into comprehension through suggestion and through teaching. But it had to be very simple at first. Will you know that the first thing I learned was how to walk! In other words, how to move as spirits move, with mental instead of physical effort. When I found I could move from place to place I was as eager and happy as a child. And this lasted quite a while, for you see I was only a child in this new life.

"Then I had to visualize differently. I had not learned the difference between physical and spiritual sight. This took longer, and meantime I made some mistakes. After that my hearing developed. I do not mean that I had no perception of what we might call hearing, but it was really thought transference or telepathy, as you might call it, from my guide. It was some time before I actually heard spirit voices. And then after a longer time, I began to hear faint sounds of music, like some far-off exquisite orchestra. I can never tell you how this affected me, nor with what joy I discovered that I was musical in my soul. That was one of the things I was denied, for the most part, in my earthly life, and I did not realize my own sensitiveness to sound, nor did I dream that sound could bring such ecstasy.

"Then I knew what I wanted to study, and after a long time spent in acquiring speech, hearing, sight, and movement, I took up that study in earnest. I loved it and did not suppose anything could be equal in attraction. But finally my guide called me to go with her to meet others who had come over as ignorant and as helpless as I had been, and suddenly my heart was touched, and my love went out to them without effort. So these two were my regular occupations; and later I added astronomy to a degree, never to a proficiency; and after that, travel.

"I had really not cared for a home at that time. I went from hall to hall, temple to temple, seeking knowledge. And not until Dee came, and our love wished an abiding place that we might call home, did I begin to think of architecture.

"Dee will tell you the rest."

'Can you tell us how you came to be leader of that circle?'

51

"Well, I was so eager for knowledge that perhaps I gained faster than others. Then my work with the newly arrived souls, many of whom longed only for knowledge of their friends, and to send word to them of their safety, made me begin to study communication—to add that to my other occupations. I found in this work so many ways through which I could give comfort, that I grew more and more interested. And gradually others who were attracted to the subject gathered about me, until we simply became a circle. As I had studied the subject more than the others, the leadership was left to me. And so you see it was very simple. All a matter of attraction and congenial thought."

"Then your circle is primarily one for communication?"

"Yes, that is the main work of this circle. But we are not confined to the one study. You will find great diversity of study and tastes and acquirement when you come, and will realize that through variety we avoid anything like monotony."

'Now Dee, we want you to go on with the story.'

"I will begin with our home-making. Mary came near to being just pure intellect before I arrived. But she found her heart then, and our companionship was ideal from the first. I wanted a home. She did not at first care for it, but now loves it as much as I.

"We decided upon the architecture, and wished rooms enough for friends; and, of course, I wished pictures and books and beauty in every part of the home. We planned it together. And when you come, you will find in it what I desired on earth—beauty, rest, books, music, halls for entertaining others, and quiet places for those who wish for quiet. The setting is in a grove, and I know you will love it as we do."

'As you do not need kitchens, dining-rooms, or bedrooms, just what use do you have for a home?'

"We go there for the comfort of companionship. I mean quiet companionship; for our homes are as sacred to our personality as an earthly home. No one intrudes, no crowds gather; but quiet companionship is there, and the many things we love—books, music, pictures, rest, or the entertaining of friends. Nothing is lacking except those things necessary to mortal comfort or convenience."

'Just how do you entertain? You do not play cards or give afternoon teas, do you?'

"Mary says: The manner of entertaining is as diverse as personality. Some have readings, some have artistic scenes, or you might almost say, dramas. Others at times give pure fun-loving entertainments, and all is well, and everyone happy!"

'Do you have great dramas?'

"Will you know that the great actors still give great impersonations. And, indeed, much history is told in that way. Shakespeare wrote historic plays, and actors here are greatly in demand for historic representations."

For lack of a better place in the book to put it, I will include here a paragraph on Art that was given us.

"Art is a big subject here, for it embraces all beauty, as well as all combinations of beautiful material. The beauty of art is the beauty of production; and you must remember that the natural beauty you love on earth, is here one of the arts of this life. Scenery, mountain, stream, forest, vale, and hill; beautiful homes, beautiful statuary, paintings, libraries; and even the colors and the garments we wear, and the dresses we fashion, are all in the way of art.

"Can you see what art means in this spirit life, when the touch of spirit, like a fairy wand, can create the most marvelous beauty and the finest adornments? We can call them into being and preserve them as we choose, and can scatter them to make way for other beauty.

"This all takes study. Each and every one is a class, a school, a craft by itself, and the students of that craft or school prepare themselves by education in the ways necessary for each work."

8

LANGUAGE AND SPEECH

~

W E are so accustomed to speech in our everyday intercourse, that the possibility of a more rapid means of communication seldom engages our attention. So it was with much interest that the following was received:

"Mind moves here with a quickness not to be expressed in words. We use pictures and symbols largely, because a thought can be more quickly expressed in that way. And we have trouble at all times with earth language, and particularly when trying to express spiritual conditions. But all are taught to speak the earth language so that we may help those who are there.

"We do not need to talk to convey our ideas, but we can speak whenever we wish, and oratory and poetry and lessons are given in word language. But in ordinary intercourse ideas flash from mind to mind without need for words. We speak with spirit organs as we use other spirit perceptions, and our language is beautiful and the speech musical."

This was all noted in our record, but among the hundreds of pages of other matter it was for the time lost sight of, and though some reference was made to telepathy two or three times, it so happened that speech was not mentioned. One evening Mary said:

"We can give you a few sentences if you like, from one who has just wandered into the circle to try to communicate. I will do the writing. He says that he is not gifted in expression, and has not been here long enough to acquire the eloquence of the spirit language, but he would like to convey a thought to earth for those who are listening for heavenly words."

Now this is hardly the place or occasion for this appeal, but I am after the closing sentence of this quotation as an illustration, and the plea is so earnest that I am including the whole of it. He said:

"Go forward! Let nothing discourage or keep you back. Tell the truth; plant the seed, by wayside, in desert place, or in fertile ground, and trust to the harvest to win souls into the truth. The truth is more beautiful than I can express. If only a tithe of it could be comprehended by earth mortals, the world would be fair indeed, and sin would soon fade from sight. This is the truth to spread abroad. Do not be discouraged though you seem to fail. The harvest will surely come and souls will be led into righteousness and will forget to do evil. Children will be brought into loving service, ministers will stop arguing about creeds and will teach the love and patience of Christ. Can you visualize a world in which the spirit life shall be the goal, and service to others the ordinary way of living? Go forward, I say, again and yet again! Go forward!"

"Mary says: He is in earnest and realizes the need of earth. He was not a minister on earth, but nevertheless a worker for right living and right thinking, and the knowledge acquired here has made him still more earnest."

'Does he hear what we say?'

"Yes, he hears fairly well, and I have told him some of your discouragements. You see, we can convey thought so quickly, that I could tell him of these things even while writing."

It was this idea that led me to again ask: 'Do you have anything analogous to spoken language?'

"Yes, and yes again! We have speech and plenty of it! But if thought flashes from soul to soul without speech, then it is quicker than any words, is it not? The spirit language is more in thought than in sentences. For instance, you may realize how at times a thought may suggest to you an entire picture, or an entire subject. Thus it is with us. Thought moves quickly and catches the sense of the expression before an entire sentence could be formed. This, however, might not apply to scientific explanations; nor perhaps to deep philosophy, when great accuracy would be necessary."

'Then how would you express an abstract statement?'

"That would depend upon the subject to be explained. A word might answer, or a book of explanations might happen to be the way."

'How would you convey the idea of goodness, for instance?'

"An action of goodness or kindness might be expressed pictorially; the abstract virtue would require longer definition.

"Our language is one of exceeding exactness, as well as of great beauty. There is nothing of the human language with which to compare it. You remember how I tried to give you some semblance of a spirit word, and utterly failed? So, we cannot give you our expressions; but you must take it for granted that language here is the highest type of expression, both in beauty and in its power of conveying thought."

'On arriving there do you learn it as we would learn a new language here?'

"We learn it, but not by the old slow methods of earth life. We absorb it as a flower absorbs dew, or the earth absorbs rain."

'When we arrive we will have to learn it then before we can understand much?'

"You will know from the first that love and kindness are here and surrounding you. Then you will know the words that express them. Afterward other thoughts will express themselves to you by the attitude or movement of friends, even as a child learns its mother's motions and expressions. And so, with a quickness you can hardly realize, you will acquire the language of this sphere. It grows, and grows rapidly. Can you understand?"

'Does a knowledge of languages here aid one after arriving there?'

"I do not think so. Thought telegraphs to thought and the language matters little. Consider the power of thought impressions even when not connected with language. Animals have this sensitiveness well developed, and many humans are also sensitive to thought waves."

While assembling the matter for this book, Mary and Dee have asked occasionally about our progress, and when one time I mentioned the title of this chapter, Mary added the following:

"The language here is partly symbol, partly flashes of thought or perception. These are beside and beyond our spoken language, which is more eloquent and of wider range than any known on earth. Our speakers are numerous in the halls of learning, and convey knowledge in wonderful terms. Yet always there are suggestions that arouse pictures or thought in the mind. We listen to eloquence that is thrilling, and we listen to statements that are so clear and terse that we cannot fail of understanding."

I asked if their language had changed as had ours through the passing centuries, or was it the same it had always been.

"Language is capable of expansion, and our language grows and becomes more rich as it seeks to interpret new thought and wider experience. Memory does not let go as easily here as there, and while we add new expressions, we keep the old ones too. You have almost an entire change in the English language since the early poets. We have not changed in that way because our construction is more perfect to start with. Any change is more in the expression, to take in new thought and new experience, like travels to other planets, or growing in touch with other lives or other speech."

It was in the first place a little surprising to learn that one would need to know a different language in the spirit world, but an additional surprise came when we found there were still other languages. A friend said:

"I am trying to learn the language of the different spheres that I may understand the expressions of those on higher planes."

'Is there a different language on each plane?'

"Yes, it takes on more delicate shadings; a more ethereal quality perhaps might express it, as it deals with more ethereal things. These languages are translated by the different messengers. We need to know the manner of expression to translate their words into something meaning as nearly as possible the same. Our language is not capable of expressing their finest shades of meaning. And if we of this sphere cannot translate it into adequate expression, what can mortal language do? I tell you, my friend, only a tithe of the higher teachings can get through our duller comprehension! Therefore I study and hope to be able to understand at least, whether I can give out the ideas to others in language eloquent enough or forcible enough to express what they wish to say."

A messenger spoke of the need for further knowledge of languages as follows:

"There are worlds not so immersed in material thought as the earth; worlds where spirit predominates, and where communication with the unseen becomes a natural occupation with the people. It is one of our delightful tasks to go to such worlds to give and receive information. To make more easy such communication is part of our work, for language differs, and signs and symbols often have to be used. Yet when spirit predominates comprehension is easy without any language, just a reception of the idea without any spoken word."

The difficulty of expression was again mentioned when we read one evening the beautiful sonnet that is attributed to the spirit of F. W. H. Myers:

A SONNET*

To all who wait, blindfolded by the flesh.
Upon the stammered promise that we give,
Tangling ourselves in the material mesh
A moment, while we tell you that we live,
Greeting, and reassurance; never doubt
That the slow tidings of our joyful state,
So hardly given, so haltingly made out,
Are but the creaking hinges of the gate.
Beyond, the garden lies; and as we turn,
Wond'ring how much you hear, how much you guess,
Once more the roses of glad service burn
With hues of loving thought and thankfulness;

---

* From the book, *Christopher* by Sir Oliver Lodge. Published and copyrighted by George H. Doran Company, 1919.

Once more we move among them, strong and free,
Marveling yet in our felicity.

"The poem is true. If only you could see our difficulty of expression you would be patient with misunderstandings. We are not so in touch with material language and thought as to be able to express the marvels of this life by material words or imagery. We are of different conditions and different expression, yet we try to become material for the moment, that we may help you to understand; but often the language fails and we are confused by lack of right words."

I don't remember now what made me ask the following question, but I do remember the surprise with which I received the reply. I asked Dee:

'Are you known by your old name there?'

"No. I have another name here. But with earth friends I keep the earth name."

'Are all names different there?'

"We all have different names here, but we love to hear the old familiar names from friends there. We take names more suitable for ethereal qualities."

We asked what determined the name.

"Names here apply to character more than to fancy, and we know each other by some distinguishing characteristic. But all names are musical and good to hear."

'But you are all good and are all perfect, so it would seem that you would all have the same names?'

"No. That is your conception of this life, but you are far from comprehending. Personal characteristics are as pronounced here as they are there, except that we do not have the distinction of being 'faulty' or 'awkward' or 'homely' or 'sinful' as people on earth might have, if called by their distinguishing characteristics."

'I should think that you would run out of names in so great a multitude?'

"You do not realize the variety of attributes here. But even so, think how many there are of the same name on your plane. It does no harm to have the same name repeated here anymore than it does there."

I asked what my name would be, and was told:

"We will not tell you, though we think we know it already."

'Who gives it to me?'

"It grows. It is written all over you!"

I was talking at one time through the pencil with my father. I felt that he would get great pleasure in the wonderful opportunities for knowledge, and he assured me that this was so, and spoke of the great libraries there:

"You will never be happier than when you see the wonderful libraries and the wonderful knowledge expressed in them. Different from earth libraries, but the word may express what I mean."

'Can you give us any impression of how knowledge is thus stored?'

"It is all so intangible to your way of expression, I do not know that I can describe it. But if you can picture wireless telegraphy as impressing itself in words then can be read—if you can think of thought expressing itself almost simultaneously, flashing itself on pages, perhaps you can get an idea of the way books are formed. There are such great minds here, and the greatest of earth's writers find their powers so exalted and so easily expressed, that books may appear without labor. We have libraries, and there are books and books, and knowledge comes easily to those who seek. Clairvoyance might express it somewhat—an illumination that presents the thought without effort. This on the part of the reader. The writer gives his thought inspirationally, and the words are transferred to the page without effort.

"Something like this. I cannot give any more definite description in your language."

Later Mary contributed a little to the subject as follows:

"We have books, or the spirit counterpart of books. They are composed of etheric substance, but can be read by spirit sight, and enjoyed by the students and teachers here. They are not quite as earth books are, but are still something within the touch and sight of spirit, and can be read at any time. How could we store up the histories of worlds, or the progress of other planet life, if we only saw the present? Our teachers of history are wonderful in their learning and their memory, but they prepare the lessons given to others from the books that are within the reach of all in the libraries here."

9

SPIRIT LIFE

⁓

WITH most people the mind is so completely ruled by the material senses that they are almost incapable of conceiving or understanding spirit life in any way. Any idea of life without material bodies is almost unthinkable. The effort to bring such a conception within the bounds of comprehension is so great that no doubt it is a factor, and possibly a large one, in making the general public inclined to shy at any mention of spirits. The prospect of mental effort is apt to make most of us wary in approaching subjects requiring much thought.

One's thought about a spirit being is apt to be confused with impressions formed by ghost stories—something unreal, something to be doubted, because contrary to our usual sense conceptions. I presume we must have expressed some such impression to cause the following to be written:

"I am here just as surely as you are there, and more so; because I am all that life can give, and you still have the limitations of material life, which prevents the fullness of spiritual expression."

'But you do not seem real?' we said.

"Reality is something that exists. We exist, mind exists, and all the things created by mind exist as long as the mind holds them in existence. We exist, but not in material form. But spirit is higher in the scale of existence than matter; therefore, we are more real than we were in our material forms. Life here is reality, and we have spiritual forms far better than the earthly ones. All the finer qualities of mind and soul are expressed by us in greater degree than before we lived the spiritual life.

"There is no life but spirit anywhere in the universe, but the material envelope in which it is enclosed oftentimes hinders free expression. We are trying to free the spirit a little from its earthly encumbrances and let it see its destination out among the stars."

'Can you tell us of your life there?'

"Life here is sane and normal, and any other description is an injustice. But we are not here for amusement, though we may be amused. We are here for knowledge and work: knowledge of spiritual conditions, work for the earth people that they may learn these conditions."

'Do you have no pleasures?'

"Do you think that the things that influence you there, such as music and all that brings you inspiration, are not the things that give us happiness here? Have you any conception of what the music of this life could be? As to pleasures—pleasure of companionship here is largely dependent on congeniality as it is there. Do not think that arrival here causes lives to be suddenly transformed. Life is a growth here as there. Happiness is a relative term.

"All human faculties are here spiritualized and enlarged. We are given the finest education in all conceivable lines, and thus fitted for helping others. With spiritual power comes occupation in the highest sense, for we become teachers and lead others along the paths we have already followed. Some are fitted for one work, some for another; but all are in happy and congenial employment. This is our work; pleasure is work, and work is pleasure. But we have many pleasures besides; you might say, earth's highest pleasures idealized.

"For heaven is real and earth the shadow; spirit the reality and matter the unreality.

"Worth is of more value than beauty; but worth expresses itself in beauty. When the spirit first arrives it is not more beautiful than the earth life expressed, but becomes beautiful in proportion to spiritual advancement. All spirits are fairer than their earthly envelope, and increase in beauty as the spirit progresses.

"Life is good when character is good, but not when character is evil. We must overcome evil and change it into good. That is our mission."

'If all become perfectly good, it would almost seem as though life would become monotonous?'

"We have more varieties of goodness than the mortal life can show. You will be surprised at the difference in individuals on a plane where none are perverse or wicked. Then think of the different occupations and industries, the different arts and sciences, of travel to other worlds and the wonders revealed there. Think of oratory, music, poetry, and the light and winsome touches that writers of humorous literature have brought to this side; and you will realize a little how, instead of monotony, we have infinite variety."

We had been asking some rather deep questions about life in general, and a teacher came one evening with the following in answer:

"Life is an unknown quantity. Even we here do not analyze, nor control, nor dissect, nor understand. It is! That is all. Now what are we to do with it? Earthbound minds are dealing with earthly materials: money, food, dress. But all of these are like vanishing shadows to us. What then shall we do with this wonderful extension of our powers and existence? Forever! Think of it! To go on and on! How?

"Let me try to tell you of the 'how' as it seems to us.

"You have already had glimpses of our activities, but only glimpses. It is not possible to outline perfectly all of our interests and work. They are wide as the universe, as different as the thought of man or spirit.

"Wonder upon wonder, marvel upon marvel, unfold to our growing vision, and life is never for one instant lacking in interest. Nevertheless it is best to focus our attention, study, and thought on those things most interesting to each personality. Some choose science, some philosophy, some invention, some the studies of other universes and other lives. The thought of this circle is directed in various ways, with Mary, your instructor, as our leader. She wishes us to come in contact with earthly minds, and help those minds to greater influence through spiritual guidance. Therefore one of our activities is, as you know, communication with earth. This is only one of several, however. Mary is also interested in sound vibrations, therefore music is one of our studies, as well as one of our pleasures.

"And I wish I could take you out with us sometime when we are far away in the study of astronomy. We can see far more with spirit sight than even the perfected instruments of human wisdom and learning can discern. Then we can travel, as no mortal can conceive, and we can study at first hand some of the problems of other planets and other lives. This is one more activity. But do not think that our studies stop here. The history of life on the other planets, for instance, is very absorbing.

"If anyone feels impelled to take up any study, he is not held back from progress. No one is limited in time or opportunity. If it can come within the scope of this circle, well and good. If more can be learned elsewhere, the student is free to go. Love and friendship prevail everywhere, and the best good of all is the one idea for all. We have no limits to our hopes nor our opportunities, as I said. Help us from your side to realize and make actual the communication between the two worlds."

We spoke one evening of the number in the circle with whom we had talked, and were told there were still some whom we did not know, but who were getting acquainted with us rapidly. We replied rather lightly that we doubted if that profited them much. Mary quickly responded:

"If they are satisfied you ought to be. You can be very nice— and you can be very bad: that is when you doubt us and will not let us come. But we take you as you are, and hope you will take us in the same way.

"We are not saints by any means—just mortals, with the mortal part mostly eliminated and something a little finer in its place. But this something finer must grow through discipline and education even as it did on earth; and we are trying to help you to begin your education now, so that you will not have such a weary way to travel here as many earth lives do.

"We are here in the room with you and can see you plainly; only we see your soul lives far plainer than your physical ones. But we are glad of that, for so we see the beautiful part of your spirit lives that are coming to us later."

We had been told much of the future life, but found we had nothing of life's origin. Our various questions brought out the following:

"What is life? We do not know! It is! It is like the answer we have to give in regard to the Supreme Deity: It is! That is all we know. What this most subtle, most unseeable, most elusive No, we cannot discover it. It simply is! That is all. Some philosophers and scientists may think they know, but they do not. It is the riddle of the universe, and only the Creator of the universe holds the secret in his soul."

"All life is of spirit origin though manifesting itself in such manifold and even grotesque forms. The wide diversity comes from the material envelope, and in what Darwin called adaptation to environment. Spirit is indestructible, not subject to disease or death. But the earthly form in which for a time it manifests itself, may be subject to all the accidents and disease of mortal existence.

"I do not know all universes, nor all the ways of life in them; but I think all immortal spirits are always first in human form, and subject to material conditions, and come out of these conditions according to the laws of spiritual evolution. Life here is still progressing to higher forms, and will finally reach a perfection as yet undreamed even by us of the lower planes."

I asked about the origin of individual life.

"Your individual life commenced with your soul or spirit, which holds the germ of immortal life. The germ of that soul may have started far back, even in the animal creation. But germs are not souls and the animal is not the man. For all practical purposes, and for all knowledge of life as we see it, your individual life commenced with your birth. To go back of that leads into such obscurity and confusion that it is hardly worthwhile."

This reply did not satisfy our curiosity, and shortly afterward we asked Prof. James of our origin. Where were we before birth?

He replied rather decidedly:

"Give it up. We have to. There is a limit to our knowledge for which we at present ought to be thankful."

But we persisted in our query and again asked Mary about individual life. Where did it come from?

"Where did it come from? What did you hear once of the germ of life and its first entrance into the human? It may have been long on its way, but at last it reached the ultimate of earth existence."

'I meant a certain individual life?'

"Well, the individual life comes from human lives immediately preceding it, and is perhaps not so much of a spiritual problem as you think; simply the process of creation which is part of the law of human existence laid down for earthly progeny since the beginning of this mortal existence."

'You mean that it is just a human creation?'

"Just that. It is part of the life germ as it pertains to human existence. I believe that once an individual human life is started it persists through all eternity. But the subject is so big that I would rather leave it for other teachers to express."

The next evening she said:

"I was thinking of that germ of life proposition, and wish to state it differently. I think that the life force is a part of the individual at all times, and the life force of the parents simply appears in a new expression; the same as seed puts forth plant, leaf, flower, and seed, to spring again in another form, yet bearing the marks of its progenitors."

We asked about the continuance of unborn lives. We had been told that they persisted.

"That is the truth that is generally accepted by us of this plane. But you must remember that we are not conversant with all the problems of all the truths made known to more advanced students. We learn much, but each circle takes up different studies largely of their own choosing. I have not been particularly interested in the query of the 'whence' as you put it; the 'whither' attracts me more."

One evening we asked a teacher from a higher plane to tell us something of life on those planes.

"We learn of the higher powers and studies, and we are here to tell others what we have learned. This we are always glad to do for those who are truly interested.

"Come with me and see the life on a higher plane. No jar or discord to mar the perfect joy of life. All are occupied with the perfecting of many new ideas and many new forms of activity; ever increasing knowledge and joy in service. You know to a certain extent of the occupations, but there are others more ethereal in character given to the more advanced powers.

"Millions of worlds are needing help, and our higher spirits are sent in as many directions as the needs require. Millions of needs require millions of activities, and teachers are coming and going constantly from world to world, from universe to universe, with helpful forces of thought and spirit control. For in many of the outlying planets mind is not so dense as upon the earth, and the spiritual impression can be sent to the thought to manifest outwardly in action."

These teachers are interested in other worlds as they say, but the list evidently includes our own, for one of them spoke as follows:

"I am here from another plane, and wish to say a few words for earth people to hear. Will you tell them that spirit is the only life; and the nearer they come to spiritualizing the earth life; the nearer they come to us. Will you tell them that the need of the world lies in spiritualizing all earth life, and bringing the Christ love to be the rule of life."

To show that we might do more than is done in spiritual development, one of these teachers told us of the power of thought:

"Thought is the force, the power here that creates. With this marvelous power we can surround ourselves with the environment we wish, create the conditions we wish, and so progress or retard our lives as we wish.

"The parallel of this power exists in mortal will and mortal thought, and if studied, directed, and persistently used, is capable of enlarging all mortal power, increasing all mortal success, and enhancing all mortal happiness."

The power of thought through suggestion was spoken of one evening rather unexpectedly. Dee wrote:

"There is one here who is listening to words from earth, and he thinks we are not making clear enough the power of spirit to manifest itself upon human character. He says:

"Remember the spirit, the immortal you, is ever present, ever ready to receive suggestion. Have a care, you people of earth, that you do not stifle this voice from heaven, for through the spirit the heavenly life may be begun on earth."

'But we are told that the spirit is not always good?'

"That is true, yet even then it can be trained to receive the education from here. I would save all criminals, even degenerates, through suggestion to their souls. It can be done, for I tried it while on earth."

'Are you a hypnotist?'

"No, not that; but one strongly impressed with the power of suggestion. It might be well to hypnotize criminals at first, but the suggestion can be made otherwise. Sleep is nature's way of rendering the human mind passive, and this condition might well be used to bring the soul of the criminal into higher thought."

'We have been reading a message from that side stating that we are born with quality of consciousness, and some possibly have so little that no improvement is possible?'

"Yes, we know that, too. But that is no reason for supposing that all are lacking quality, and because of this, other environment and other influence should be tried. Will you give this emphasis in your book?"

'Can you tell us who you are?'

"I am a teacher who is studying here as I studied there, the best way of turning evil into good, or rather, effacing evil by good."

'Did you use suggestion when here?'

"I used it there and had success with it. I belonged to the French school of thought at Nancy, and other experimental places. What the work did for the undeveloped and the subnormal and the criminal, I can never forget; and I wish to give it such emphasis from here that it shall gain prominence there."

'Do you use it on that side?'

"Yes, we use it and we accomplish much. But we lack one condition that the human life has that is a help, and that is sleep."

After reading some poetry for a time one evening, Sis took up the pencil, and Mary immediately wrote:

"I never read poetry on earth, but you are living poetry now, and so am I. The perfect whole of existence, the final harmony, and the outlook beyond— it is all so wonderful and so satisfying! You do not comprehend as we do, but your vision is growing and will continue to grow until you are conscious of the perfect plan of existence. You can only see pieces there, and many very poor pieces; but from here we can discern the whole, though we are not yet living the whole of life. Try to live in the glimpses that give you even vague outlines of this life."

At another time she spoke further:

"The life you are now living is but a shadow of the real—the earth experience as compared to this life. We are trying to show you the reality, but impressions are hard to give. The impressions you have received are for the most part true, but the reality is so incredibly more beautiful that we cannot make the impression convey to you a true picture of the reality.

"If the earth people only knew of the riches of the spirit life which they might inherit if they would, the earth life would become spiritualized and all suffering and hardship would end. All realize it at last, but why waste years and years sometimes, many lifetimes even, before they come to the true spirit life! You may think it enough that at last they do come to the truth, but if you could see the wasted lives and wasted time here, you would desire as fervently as we to hasten the day of their spiritual birth. For of a truth, one must be born into the spirit when earth life has so submerged the spirit that it has almost been lost."

'God is all-powerful,' we said, 'why were we not created good to begin with?'

"It is of no use to ask why. We do not know. There are many things that we do not comprehend. But we live in the midst of such advanced and beautiful lives, that we find it easy to trust. Also the teachers from the higher planes help us to realize the infinite progression and the infinite goodness, so we trust and grow happy as we grow in faith.

"We see what you see of the terrible atrocities and suffering on earth, and help where we can, and trust for the rest. The worst cruelties have their limit, for human life ceases when too hard to be borne. And when they arrive here—the innocent suffering ones— they are met with peculiar tenderness, and every effort is made to make up to them for the horror and suffering they have endured."

We spoke one evening of the difficulty of convincing some who were always putting forth some new theory to account for spirit manifestation.

"Human mind reasons from the material aspect, and it is hard to overcome the logic of that viewpoint, for the spiritual aspect is so beyond all material conception that the human mind stumbles into false reasoning in trying to judge of its future.

"That is not as I wished to phrase it, but as near as you can get it now.

"It is knowledge of the truth that we wish to give you, that the close of the earth life may be filled with joyous anticipation rather than fear. Take life as a heavenly gift, both here and there, and know that leaving that life is only a change from a lower into a higher grade; but with such rich advantage as can never be described. Be happy. Let the future be filled with joyous anticipation. Do the good you can there, and be ready to go on doing good here in the happiest possible way, under incomparably happy conditions."

I said I knew that it would all be arranged somehow, but I did sometimes wonder how I, who did not like crowds, could manage there, where people seemed to form so much of life.

"We are not obliged to be continually with people," Dee answered. "We meet together for work or teaching, but we may be alone, or with intimate companionship of dear friends when we wish. Nothing is forced on us. We are led to the conditions that are best for our development, and these form our joy as well. You are bound by the knowledge of earthly needs and limitations. But we are free from these and free to choose our occupations. Sissy used to say she would like to be on a cloud and drift slowly through the sky, and something like that still pleasure might be hers here, only not as she expressed it. That was a picture of rest in her mind, and rest was what she needed. The same need or desire here would find perfect fulfillment. That is all."

Sis said she enjoyed so many things here, she wondered if she would not miss some of them there.

"Don't worry! You will find the counterpart of every pure joy here, and in greater measure than we can express. Never fear. All the joys that you have there will only be intensified here."

Sis asked if she would be able to enjoy these at first, or would she be some time in learning.

"Mary says: There are some things that you will have to wait to understand, but you must take our word for it that they exist. Dee has told you that she has never a regret for the earth life and the beauty she left there. All is more than equaled here. Let this fill your heart and mind with joy."

We had been reading a description of the spirit life that did not appeal to us. It was given as a symbolic vision. Mary replied to our inquiries:

"Your thought brings you the truth that appeals to you, but it is the truth just the same. Heaven is an unlimited space and there is room for many ideals. But you will be happier if you hold fast to the truth that appeals to you, for it is the truth. Never doubt that.

"Many here express truth pictorially or symbolically, but the real truth is the word that describes the life without embellishment or picture. The book you speak of will attract a certain type of mind, yet other minds would be repelled by such a description. Each in his own way. Can you not see? No matter how earth people are drawn into the spirit comprehension, whether by symbol, poetic fancy, or simple description, it will be all right when they arrive here. We are telling you the simple truth, and you may take it to your inmost heart and take the comfort of it. You will never be disappointed, while some others may have to begin all over again in their comprehension of this life."

Sis and I were talking one evening about the life there, and of the difficulty of our finite minds' grasping it. When the writing was begun, Dee said:

"You get now and then vague ideas or pictures of the comfort and pleasure of this life; but the reality has not entered into your real understanding yet. Sissy is afraid she will have to go on to a higher plane when she doesn't wish to; is afraid she will not be quite contented here, and will miss some of the surroundings or friends or pleasures of the earth life. She will not! That is all I can say."

Sis laughingly replied that she would miss the picnics.

"You can have one then! You are a bad child and don't deserve all you will get; but it will be yours anyway, picnic and all."

Many people have communicated with us, and through the pencil to others. One who passed over as an old man was talking with his grandson. Closing the conversation he said:

"The tie between the two worlds, or rather the one world of the seen and the unseen, grows closer as the years go by. I did not know much about this life when there, but I imagined more than I knew. The normal life here was a surprise; for I had thought of angels with wings and harps, and heaven as a city of golden streets. But nothing of the kind is here. Normal progression; friends, work, service for others— yes! happiness, in travel, music, books, and congenial companions.

It is all normal and all true. It is worth working for there. And all the work is simply to have high ideals and live up to them. The golden rule is no dead letter. Be sure of that!"

I spoke one evening of that being my birthday. Mary responded:

"What of it! You will have millions of them!"

Then in a moment she went on:

"We are not thinking of birth at all. It is always the present here. No looking forward to old age and decrepitude of either mind or body. The future is ours; the present is ours. How different from the half fear of the future, the dread of the years that may bring hardships, the looking forward to the silence of the grave, and the terror of the future! Can you see?

"I was not happy on earth, but I feared the end of that life, and had rather a morbid terror of death. Will you see the difference now? Nothing to fear, neither sickness, poverty, age nor death. Why count the years, when each passing one will only add to your happiness and power, and preserve forever both youth and beauty? Goodbye to birthdays; greet the future with joy that will take no cognizance of years!"

10

THE NEGATIVE ASPECT OF
SPIRIT LIFE

~

PROBABLY very few people have really tried to analyze the conditions, and tried to determine what activities and occupations engage the time and attention of the inhabitants of the spirit world. When one realizes that there are no material bodily requirements whatever in the spirit life, and when one really comprehends what a gap would be left in our life here if all such activities were unnecessary, it opens up a whole new field of thought. The subject of what one would not find or need there— what one might call the negative aspect of spirit life—was brought up for Mary's comments, and a copy of our record for that evening is here given. Sis and I had talked of it a little, and when I turned to Mary, I said:

'In the first place, you have no day and no night, and no divisions of time.'

"No day and no night and no divisions of time, you say. We have the divisions of work and study and recreation and quiet hours or times for ourselves. Do you not divide your days by actions rather more than you think? There are the meal times, the work times, the play times, and the resting times. That is very similar to our divisions."

'Yes, but you do not reckon time by hours and minutes.'

"Hardly. We have a system or order of work and study, though what you call hours and minutes are not so counted by us. The divisions of time are not arbitrary, but I am thinking how to tell you of the orderly way in which we work. Perhaps if I call it (this by way of illustration) a central office, where the plans of work are arranged and messengers sent to us when we are needed, it may help you a little."

'Well, again: You have no need for food, and so no rivalry in obtaining it; no buying or selling, no business of any kind, no money, no medium of exchange.'

"We are as busy as you. We exchange many things, which might be called barter. For instance: I study something I wish to perfect myself in, and teach, perhaps, my very teacher in some other branch. We exchange many things, sometimes work, sometimes ideas, sometimes the many acts of love or friendliness; but all without your medium of exchange, money. We have love instead, or, if to those we do not know, whatever courtesy suggests. So you see we have a busy trading system, and enjoy it too, and no one becomes bankrupt."

Sis said it was very difficult for her to realize that there would be no desire to eat or sleep.

"You will never miss either. Instead, you will be delighted that the sordid occupations of life do not interfere with your progress."

'So much of life here is made up of chasing the dollar with which to buy food and comfort, it would seem that many people would be completely lost over there. What will a banker do there, for instance?'

"Will you know that his training there will not be lost here. He may not handle money, but there are many other ways in which that trained accuracy will be of service."

'Then, your travel is so different. You have no railroads, no trains, no automobiles, no airplanes, no steamships.'

"Wait till you come and we take you on a trip to some far-off place. The mode of travel will be as much finer, as your Cadillac is finer than a wheelbarrow!"

'Having no need of the things that money buys, there can be with you no jealousies because of place or position attained by material blessings.'

"They who serve most are the greatest here. There is no computing of place or position except by service or wisdom. Service may be of the intelligence, or of the spiritual gifts, or the more common activities; but the wiser the service, or the more loving and unselfish the giving of one's self—these are the things that give prominence in spirit life."

'You have no thieves or robbers, and no need for insurance policies.'

"We have the unworthy ones to guide and the wicked ones to convert, and the time and patience given to this work is more than any occupation on earth would probably demand. The unworthy ones are always with us, therefore that work is never done."

I said they had no color line, therefore no race prejudice, and Sis asked if spirits were always white.

"Not that exactly, but spirit is not black or red or yellow or brown. It is spirit, that is all."

When we read this later, Mary corrected it by saying:

"That would seem to make spirit a colorless substance. That would be quite the opposite of the truth. Spirit is white, in a way, because spirit represents truth, beauty, and nobility of character. The character determines the exterior, and purity of soul expresses itself in purity of appearance."

'Then, as you have remarked several times, you have no care of the house or clothing or person?'

"It makes us almost weary to think of all these things; but your list has brought to our attention our freedom and our joys. We become so accustomed to our blessings that we perhaps forget a little, and it is good to be reminded."

'But, Mary, what are the youngsters going to do? There are no games of football, no baseball, no tennis, no golf, no billiards, no card-playing!'

"Don't you worry. There are pleasures beyond these, and there are delightful occupations that take the time."

Sis spoke of the wonders of mountain scenery here, and asked if any such would be there.

"What did you hear from the college professor in regard to the desires of life here? Were you not to see the rugged and the grand, as well as the quiet beauty of valley and stream? He is right, and there will be no disappointment for you."

'But the snowy mountain ranges here have an attraction just because we cannot easily reach them. Dee could there go in an instant to anything she wanted to see.'

"She would not be impressed in the way you would sense it; but it would impress her, nevertheless. You can look into fathomless space here as well as there. You can see infinite distance, and the evidences of infinite power. And you can see the wonderlands of strange planets."

Sis then spoke of the Spanish dances and the play of color in the 'Mission Play' which we had just seen.

"Will you try to imagine the grace and beauty of motion that is without fatigue, dress fairer than any the world has seen; beauty of person, of dress, of motion, and all without vanity or selfishness? You cannot get beyond earth comparisons, I know; but if your spirit sight could be clear for one minute even, you would never again believe that heaven can lose by comparison with the joys or the beauties of the world."

'Well, we have covered the ground fairly well with the negative illustrations, though no doubt it could be elaborated almost endlessly.'

"We think you are answered in a way; but one half-hour of vision, yes, even one half-minute, would be more convincing."

11

STUDY AND TEACHING

~

THE joy of acquiring knowledge is one of the delights of this life. We never tire of learning, for we love knowledge too much. It is only earth weariness that may hinder you. We learn of the stars and all the elements that compose the stars. Then all the diversified lives on the millions of planets surrounding the stars; all the products and combinations of chemical action; all the history of life from its lowest forms upward; light, electricity, sound waves, musical vibrations and the harmonies resulting therefrom; all that is beautiful in the world of art or in the world of literature. Of course not all these are studied at once nor by the same person.

"Many pleasures are here also, for there are many varieties of minds and many conditions to meet. In pleasures the reunion of friends and relatives must be counted. And there is the delight of loving friendship, and companionship higher and finer and more enduring than worldly ties. We have concerts of music that would delight your soul; and wit and eloquence are as much valued here as there. Then there is travel; for we can move slowly or fast as we choose.

"Can you realize the interests that fill our lives? Variety of occupation; all forms of beauty; friendships more dear than earth can ever know; ever increasing knowledge; music such as mortals cannot conceive; all that heart can wish or mind enjoy. If the soul asks for more, we turn to those of the next higher plane, and are given what we desire. We in turn try to help others to reach their ideals, and we are wishing now to make known to the dwellers on earth, the happy existence here, that 'death may lose its sting and the grave its victory.'"

"All knowledge here is acquired with ease, and all the spirit functions of sight, hearing and memory are vastly in advance of the earthly ability, and there is no limit to knowledge or happiness.

"After character has been established, we study for knowledge of the earth from which we here all come, knowledge of the conditions there, and ways of improving those conditions. Then the knowledge of higher spiritual activities and the power that this knowledge gives, knowledge to be used for other lives, sometimes on earth, sometimes on other planets. After this, still increasing knowledge and still increasing power for good. Always giving out. Do not forget that knowledge is to be used for others."

"The education of the soul is very complex. It has to grow in so many directions, that no one description can make it plain to you. First the sight, then the hearing. Of course these are the mediums through which knowledge is received. Then the recognition and cultivation of intuitive faculties. These are elementary and are additional methods of progress. Then comes the study of spiritual laws; for these must be known and understood, that a newly arrived spirit may not infringe upon them. These laws have to do with the harmony of heaven and the perfect accord of millions upon millions of souls. Once these laws are understood, the newly arrived spirit may discover the infinite variety of teaching here and may select the study most adapted to his taste. This does not mean ignorance along other lines, however, for education is harmonious and many-sided; but simply the specialty he desires most to perfect himself in. This done, his work commences, happy work and happy acquisition of knowledge. Always this specialty in view, yet with so many other sidelights, or occupations that the variety is always stimulating to new endeavor and further progress. Then his fitness for a teacher is decided upon, and if he has this talent he becomes a teacher of others. There is no limit to acquisition and no limit to one's taste. Two or three specialties often go together. Mary here has half a dozen. She uses these and still goes on acquiring other knowledge for her own pleasure. The one-sided person does not exist here. He would be a curiosity."

'You have some sort of government, have you not?'

"Yes, we are held to account in various ways. We receive instructions from higher intelligences, and report to them of success or failure. But there is no unreasoning tyranny, remember that. For instance, if I have a talent in someone direction, I may be asked to use that talent. Or if I need instruction in some direction, I may be asked to seek that instruction. All is meant for our development, and for our more intelligent or capable service."

'Then you have nothing that corresponds to our political government?'

"No, for all here is the process of development, and the best good is the one thought."

'How do those in authority gain their position?'

"Can you compare it with the system on earth a little? There are teachers above us who are wiser than we. They come to us to help direct our efforts. Above them are wiser ones still—I mean those who have been here longer, and have been led into higher knowledge.

It is like the grades of school, just a little. But the authority in its finality must come from an all-wise ruler whom you call God. And we look up to Christ as his representative among the spheres and circles.

"Then can you understand that the teachers come to us with the authority of goodness and purity of character, and wisdom derived from the higher influences and the higher studies? Character, wisdom, love, service—these are the characteristics of the teachers who help us, who make our laws, and lead us into the higher knowledge and service."

12

LOVE AND SERVICE

~

"NOW abideth faith, hope, love, these three, but the greatest of these is love." (1st Cor. 13:13.) "Love is the fulfilling of the law." (Romans 13:10.)

Thus wrote Paul nearly two thousand years ago. And again in this later century the lesson of love is being sent to us with renewed urgency.

"Love and service; service and love. These must be the watchwords if the world is ever to be at peace. Love is the foundation on which all goodness stands, and must in some way become the law of life everywhere. Love is one, but its manifestations appear in a thousand ways. Love is never wasted. Its influence may not be recognized, but its power is sure."

Then we are told that love and service walk hand in hand in that other and better life.

"All labor, all service, all giving of one's self, should begin with love and be filled with love, service to mankind, service always and everywhere, with love as the foundation of the effort. Christ came to preach this law of love, and the world must be rebaptized with love if it is to experience peace among nations."

So often was the necessity for love and service on earth reiterated, so often a spiritualizing of the earth life insisted, that once we asked if teaching and preaching this truth was the sum and substance of spirit life.

The answer came with emphasis and speed:

"But there is much beside preaching and teaching. Architecture, color formation, flowers and beauty of scene, studies of the heavens above and the planets revolving about their suns, the strange lives on these planets, invention, discovery. Where did the discoveries of earth come from? Did the cave dwellers know the secrets of electricity, or did they fly through the air, or sail the oceans, or live in luxurious homes? Don't forget that the impulse to these improvements came from here.

"And these impulses given to mortals are a part of the love and service that sound to you like preaching. Many material beings must be helped along material lines. The dwellers on some of the outer planets have to be inspired to find ways of obtaining heat and food. We help them to find the best of the material world in which they live.

"Can you realize how different life would be if mortals would learn to live the unselfish life, and learn also the truths of spiritual existence? There must be progress in spiritual life if the world is to be saved from becoming a wreck.

"You think we have used one expression over much: that of love and service as describing heavenly activity. But in the poverty of human expression and the lack of human knowledge of the life of the spirit, how can we better express the heavenly joy and activity?

"Do not dwell on the past. Its failures and disappointments are over. Let them go. Move onward and upward. Live in spiritual thought, in the spiritual ideals of love, joy, peace, and happiness."

13

ACTIVITIES AND OCCUPATIONS

~

MANY aspects of life in the spirit world are made more clear by what has been already said. But only a little has so far been presented that makes one familiar with their general activities—what we would speak of as their daily life and occupations. To have real happiness in the earth life one must be busy under congenial circumstances. When this rule is applied to spirit life, one at once begins to wonder what they do, how they put in the time, in a world where no hours are set aside for sleeping, eating, care of the person or care of the dwelling; or, more than all, for making a living.

Early in our writing we had been told enough to set us thinking, and we remarked:

'Your descriptions are rather different from the old ideas of psalm singing and golden streets.'

"That was a much misunderstood figure of speech. It was only a mind picture to suggest happiness and occupation; but earthly thought took it too literally."

'There was nothing else to suggest a different idea,' we replied.

"I know. That is why we want to give you greater knowledge of this life, which is as sane as the highest earthly occupation, and far more delightful."

"I can tell you some of our activities, but you may have trouble in understanding, as we cannot well express them in terms of human language. For instance, you cannot understand the terms we use in creating or combining colors. You could not possibly understand how our music is created. And so with a multitude of things.

"To tell you anything of our occupations, you must know first that we are taught to work for others, which is the joy of life here. Then we are taught various sciences and the methods of spirit thought. We are then allowed to go to other planes and study the conditions there. We can see all the life on the different planets and work there if we choose. We are free to choose our work; but, if later we find objections, we may change. Some are teachers, some are messengers, some welcome the new arrivals, many are caring for the little children, some study the other planets, and many will go to distant worlds to learn such new conditions as may be understood.

"We are interested in the development of the processes of the mind as they act upon outward things, such as the formation of our plant life, the combination of colors, and the manufacture of fabrics. These are all mind processes, all regulated by fixed laws.

"We plan the beautiful fabrics with which spirits are clothed, and it is also with the powers of the mind that homes and halls and buildings for art and teaching are constructed. Architecture is a marvelous work, and we have all the riches of heaven to inspire the planning of the wonderful buildings.

"Authors are here writing books. I mean spiritually writing them, and spiritually reading them to others. Will you be surprised to learn that writing by alphabet is taught? That is part of our education in order to keep the memory of earth language and so to communicate with those of earth.

"Some study chemistry as it pertains both to the material and to the invisible life. Others teach history. The poor little earth is not the only planet with a history! Some develop new ideas in mechanics.

Most of such things are suggested from here. Then we have work for other planets and other universes altogether away from any conditions that you know. We are in some ways more advanced than they are; in others they are superior to us. There are many problems, and in solving them we are climbing upward in many ways.

"But the way is long and the road a weary one for those who have not learned their lessons on earth. Many come here so strongly influenced by their earthly beliefs that they do not realize themselves as spirit at all, and have to be led in various ways to comprehend that death has separated them from the life they once knew. That is one of the things that give us occupation. Then we have many who have recently come over who are ignorant of this life and have to learn its new ways of perceiving and enjoying. This is another way in which some of the circle are occupied. When not engaged in helping those who need us, we are studying the spirit forces—thought power and thought building, the etheric atoms and how to use them.

"You do not know, nor can you know, all the occupations of this life. We have given you those, or described those, more nearly resembling the occupations of earth life. But there are many, many others of which you cannot as yet form any conception.

"We are active with a freedom unknown on earth because of added powers; we are happy with a joy unknown on earth because of increased sense of appreciation, and we worship with an infinitely greater reverence because we are more in touch or communion with the divine."

'Could you describe your own activities for one day?'

"Your breath would be taken away if I were to tell you of the speed and ease with which I accomplish a host of things. I may go to a planet with a message or lesson. I may go to a hall of learning; or drift away to some far-off circle to learn of its activities; or I may be helping some mortal on earth, or receiving some newly arrived soul. All of these would not be too much to accomplish in a day here, and much more could be brought within its hours if necessary."

'An intimate diary of your work, and of your impressions while doing these things, would be very interesting to mortals.'

The reply came very emphatically:

"But, you see, we do not try to keep track of what we do. That way might lead to pride. Our way is to do good and forget our work as soon as possible and move on to the next duty. But do not forget that duty and pleasure are one with us."

Considerably later, possibly a year or more afterward, we spoke of their work again, asking:

'You spoke yesterday of turning to other things after our talk. Just what did you do? And what have you been doing today?'

"Mary went to a circle where they were studying magnetic waves, and listened to a lecture on this subject. Then she went to hear some music in the great temple of music, and listened until her soul was filled with harmony. After that she went to a newly arrived spirit who was not finding her way perfectly, and tried to help her to realize her surroundings. And the hours sped by until she finally went to her home, and Dee and she had one of the dear talks and companionships which are such a blessing to them both. These are just a few things. Many others came into the day that with you is just over—such as certain other studies, journeys to the library for help and knowledge, and teachings in various ways and places."

To this I replied:

'Yes, and you did not have to do up your hair and change your dress before you went to the library; and you did not have to consider the weather; and if it was a long way, you did not have to order out the automobile, or take a street car!'

"You are right! There are no obstacles in the way, and we make each day equal to half a dozen on earth."

'What was Dee doing?'

"Mary says: She went to her children two or three times, for she has several groups under her care. Then she spent much time helping and comforting several little ones, just come over, and this is for her such a loving and lovely work. Then she went to her studies and to various lectures, and so her day passed pleasantly; and included various little occasions of going to see if you needed her and were all right. You were not well last night; but we did not worry, as we thought you would soon be better. And tonight when you took up the pencil, it seemed to be a telegram to us, and we started, one from a lecture and the other from our home, and here we are.

"Now tell us what you have been doing."

Sis said she had to see the doctor, and asked Dee if she remembered his treatments for the throat.

"I should say I did, and you hated them worse than I."

We then went over the events of the day.

"Mary says: You surely had a good time. Anything good at the movies?"

14

SPIRIT FORCES

~

A S one becomes familiar with the work of communication between the spirit and the material worlds, it is quite apparent that much difficulty is experienced when attempts are made to convey information that is beyond the ability of the medium to express.

This is illustrated when comparing our earlier communications with those of later date. When using the Ouija-board we were for a short time in touch with one who was much interested in chemistry, and he tried to give us a description of the manner in which atoms were formed. Some interesting statements were made, though little information was gained. Sis knows practically nothing of chemistry or of chemical terms. I had read a little on such subjects, so it seems likely that my mind supplied the words while my hands were on the Ouija-board. But the statements were not consciously mine, and I had previously only a vague understanding of the information conveyed. Since then, when all the communications have come through Sis's pencil, scientific subjects have not been prominent.

Persistent questioning, however, has elicited a few replies that seem important. The following was given when we were inquiring into the work of construction by "thought processes":

"We in this circle are not yet advanced enough to deal with atoms and electrons, or to watch their motions. Other planes have done this and are busy explaining the existence and movements and powers of the electrons, or 'grains of force,' as you have been told they were called. The electrons are the nearest approach to spirit of anything pertaining at all to matter. They are etherealized to such a degree as to be almost pure spirit; yet when they are surrounded by material forces they obey those laws.

"They may belong to either the seen or the unseen world. When connected with matter they become part of the material atom; when used by spirit they lose all material attractions and become amenable to spirit control."

And again:

"Try to conceive of thoughts as formative processes in themselves, and in dealing with the material used, are all-powerful to build from that material. The electrons are the material, and thought can attract, distribute, or segregate these minute particles as desired."

In talking this over, we wondered if the electron we had in mind was the same thing they mentioned. We asked Prof. James about it and he replied:

"I am not a chemist and can only answer as I have been taught by others. The electrons or 'grains of force' are scarcely differentiated from spirit. Their quality is so ethereal that spirit workers use them continually; yet they may become inherent in matter under certain conditions, and apparently become slightly material. I would call it, in the language of the psychologist, a double personality. That is hardly a fair answer to your question, but it is dealing with forces so subtle that the best of us here are simply students. The double activity is all I can use in explanation."

'You really think we are both speaking of the same thing then?'

"I imagine so, but I did not study the science of chemistry there and have no means of comparing."

The professor who long ago talked to us of chemistry added:

"The electron here is practically the same as the electron there. At least we believe so. It is the spiritual side of the material, or the material side of the spiritual force."

In studying the spirit forces it was learned that most, if not all, of them were vibratory in character. The subject of vibrations was of course quite prominent when we were told of music and its production, and some of the information concerning vibrations is included in the chapter on music.

The first mention of vibrations came very early in the communications when Dee said:

"Early in this life we are taught about chemical laws."

'What kind of chemistry have you in a spirit world?'

"I do not know how to tell you; the subject is too big for my brain."

'Do the chemical laws apply to substances unknown to us?'

"The only difference as I understand it is in the density of the substance. Density means only vibrations. These are as the vibrations of electricity and light."

After Sis had been using the pencil for some time we asked for more information concerning spirit forces, and especially vibrations. We had been talking with Mary and she said:

"We have vibrations finer and more rapid than any conceived on earth. In traveling we use different forces for different distances, and can increase the rate of speed at will."

Another teacher added:

"I can express a little of the laws of motion to you, but you must be patient with my difficulty in describing spirit laws in mortal language. Vibrations are known of course in the material world, and are studied by scientists there. But we have finer forms of these vibrations. These are as necessary to us as the lower forms are necessary to you. Could you multiply the highest vibrations there a thousand-fold, you would begin to understand the powers we use in motion, light, music, and sound."

'Is that right? Do you really mean a thousandfold?'

"We cannot state this in exact numbers, but my expression is by way of comparison and approaches the truth as nearly as I can give it."

'This is so much greater than light as we know it. Do you recognize the grades between?'

"Where earthly force ends, spirit force begins, and we are sensible of all the gradations in power and rapidity. We can control them to a large extent, and can use where we cannot control."

'We explain light as waves of ether. Are your higher forces explained in the same way?'

"Light is a part of the higher vibrations. Ether is filled with vibrations. The electrons or particles are in constant motion. We have no material substances to create vibration, as sound is created with you, but we have the finer forces of the mind."

At one time for a number of evenings a teacher from a higher plane attempted to convey to us some idea of the forces used by them. But because of the difficulty of expressing spirit powers in mortal terms, he did not succeed in getting much through concerning the forces although he did tell us of the activities on that plane.

In his talk, and in what Mary has said about spirit forces, the word electricity has been written. Regarding this, I asked:

'You have used the word electricity. Do you mean just the power we know as that?'

"No. We use the word you best comprehend. The spirit counterpart is more subtle, more ethereal, but powerful even beyond the earth-known force."

Later, when using the words magnetism and magnetic attractions, it is quite likely that spirit powers are meant rather than those we know by those names.

When the teacher was trying to describe the power of the higher plane, Sis asked:

'Has it anything to do with ether?'

"What is ether? Tell me that?"

'We cannot do that.'

"Neither can we yet. Wait until knowledge can explain more fully."

But we persisted in our questions at various times, and the following replies were elicited:

"Ether is invisible and imperishable. It is an unknown quantity filling all space. It has qualities quite unknown to mortals as yet. Higher spirits study its formation and composition and do know about it, but it is in advance of our knowledge."

'Is it possible for mortals to learn of ether, its characteristics and powers?'

"They have discovered little as yet. I think it possible; but much research work must be done first. It would be unwise for us to give such information if we knew. Study, and the desire for new truths, are for the purpose of stimulating minds on earth, and form one of the steps leading spiritward. Human understanding is slowly turning toward the spiritual; and, in some far distant time, earthly and spiritual efforts will come together, or at least the mortal may so understand the immortal, as to be nearly conformed to its spiritual counterpart."

At another time Mary said:

"The ether is the medium for the transmission of thoughts, and sometime the world will take cognizance of these silent processes and powers. But it must become more spiritualized before it understands."

It is unfortunate that Sis is not more familiar with chemistry and physics. A number of attempts have been made to describe various spirit powers, which have been partial failures because of the difficulty Sis experiences regarding the terms or vocabulary of chemistry, physics, or other scientific occupations. Several times, however, our questions have brought out a few sentences in reply, and I give some of them here. A teacher from a higher plane was talking:

"We are studying a power akin to magnetism, although it is a much finer and more spiritual force. It is produced by the action of certain etheric waves that move in circles about an etheric center. It is a force to you unknown, finer even than spirit, but so powerful that it might sway a universe."

Further regarding magnetism we were told:

"He wishes to say that the experiments of scientists are leading in the right direction, and that science will prove immortality, or rather the persistence of individual life, before long, through the study of magnetic forces."

'What do you mean by magnetism?'

"Magnetism is not an earthborn property. It is rather a spiritual substance, too fine, too ethereal, for human vision or touch. Yet it may be discovered through the action of its particles, the same as an atom may be studied without ever seeing it.

"*Magnetism is a spirit force*!

"That is enough for the present. What it does, the scientists on earth are trying to discover. When its power is known and fully understood and utilized, the bridge spanning the gulf between the mortal and the immortal will be complete."

We were talking of the book by Dr. Schrenck-Notzing of Europe, and of the forms materialized under his experimentation; and we asked if magnetism was connected with them.

"Yes; the magnetic currents flowing through the visible substance rendered it alive while it remained. But when the magnetic current was withdrawn the substance dematerialized immediately."

'You say magnetism made it alive?'

"Yes. Magnetism might be defined as life."

I asked my father one evening if he had any information for us. He replied:

"Do you keep up with the new theories in chemical science? The work is progressing here along unusual lines, and bids fair to revolutionize some of the theories over there."

I spoke of seeing an item describing how a small automobile was driven by radio electricity.

"Electricity is one of the powers closely allied with our more spiritual forces, and the study of electricity will eventually lead many into the belief in these forces. I am not a scientist myself, but I watch and wonder and admire."

Sis said she could not understand a great deal about scientific subjects.

"You will not be a scientist, I can see that. But you will use science here to help in other ways. Your music will be one of the results of science, and you will be dependent on it in a thousand ways for progress and happiness."

I said it was difficult to imagine chemical studies there, as so much of our study consisted of actual experimentation.

"You have chemical apparatus there for experiments; we have the spiritual counterparts here and through this apparatus we study along experimental and progressive lines. It is difficult for you to understand, of course; but we do experiment regarding material substances, and make discoveries of different compositions and their different uses. We know the different metals and minerals and see far ahead to a thousand uses yet unknown to mortals. There is always something to look forward to. When the earth is a worn-out magazine it will be time for mortals to quit; but that time is far away—unknown and uncounted cycles ahead."

Another evening someone else wrote:

"We are trying to get in touch with human thought and trying to influence that thought toward the pure beliefs of future life, of progress, of unselfish service. Can you help us?"

'We have had so much it would seem there was little more that was new?'

"Perhaps that is so, but 'line upon line and precept upon precept' seems to be necessary to impress the human thought. I know, for I have not forgotten my old hardness of heart concerning some things."

'Were you a religious teacher?'

"Not at all. I was a teacher of science, and that along materialistic lines. It was difficult for me to get any impression beyond the material forces. Science, you know, tries to account for all these things by material explanations. I had to come here before I found the intangible something we call spirit, or the unseen thing we know as life and immortality, or the vision that could see and accept the Divine."

'We have always been impressed by the evidence of a tendency in all life to improve—to advance.'

"That is the secret of it all—the upward climb, no matter how slow. Believe in that, and your faith will be sure. It does not need unlimited study and research in order to comprehend principles."

'But some scientists seem to think that this tendency is only another principle, another foundation law, like gravitation?'

"Who made the law? Who decided that gravitation, cohesion, magnetism, attraction, and a thousand other laws must go to the forming of a world or of a people?"

'Some think these laws always existed, were never created?'

"That is getting back into the unknowable and the unthinkable. We here do not go back farther than to the Creative Force that governs all things. Many in higher spheres have far more definite knowledge than we. Scientists on earth know nothing about it. They take their own conceptions for absolute law. But this life will disclose impressions, intuitions, as well as absolute knowledge, that will crush into nothing their manifold theories."

15

THE AURA, PERSONALITY, ETC.

~

MAGNETIC currents and magnetism lead to the subject of magnetic attraction, and this leads to personality, character, and congeniality. These determine the personal ties, the relationships, in the spirit world. There seems no dividing line. Even guardian spirits, guides, or "controls," are allied subjects for discussion.

I will begin with a remark that Mary made one evening when Sis was rather despondent, and the writing was not coming easily:

"Try to be cheerful, so that I can come into your aura, as the spiritualists say, which is only getting in touch with your mentality."

'What is the aura?'

"It is a magnetic condition which throws off certain colors in certain personalities. There is an attraction in each person's aura that calls persons of responsive attraction. You must know that there is as much difference in personality here as there. Attraction from one may not mean attraction from all. It is a matter of congeniality and sympathy, largely."

This question of attraction made me wonder whom I would have for friends over there.

"You will find those who belong in your magnetic current."

'I doubt if I have any magnetic current.'

"Everyone has it. That is the aura, so much talked about."

'Can you see the aura?'

"I see it, but I see the spirit more plainly. The aura seems like a filmy veil to me. Others see it as a thicker cloud surrounding and enveloping the individual. But it is with each one of you, and is an introductory knowledge of the spirit within. The aura carries with it the personality. It may be thick and black with criminals; it may be as beautiful as a sunset cloud; or it may be like a delicate veil; differing with different personalities."

We were talking about a young man there who was concerned because his mother here continued to grieve for him. We asked if he could see her.

"He is not clairvoyant yet as to earthly surroundings and cannot see his mother except as she draws him to her by her thought of him. You little realize what a magnetic current lies in thought, from earth to heaven, and from heaven to earth. You think of us, and we feel the thrill and answer by our presence, though you are so rarely conscious of it. This young man's mother thinks of him and her love goes out to him, and then suddenly he is near her, and recognizes her presence. He also thinks of her at times and this keeps alive her memory of him. Can you see the way in which spirit wireless messages come and go?"

'Are you compelled to come when we call?'

"We are not obliged except by the love we have and the interest we feel. When you wish to write, the effort to bring us in touch with you is like an electric signal; and whenever I feel the signal I come flying home to know what you have to say. The signal is like a flash of intelligence in the brain, or like a touch, or a sound—but anyhow we cannot mistake it however it comes. We listen, or feel, whichever way you can understand it, and come at once. You are our charge; therefore we come when you call. Also, we are watching to get our messages through to earth."

This attraction of thought was illustrated once when Mary asked Sis:

"Think of the name of some person here, and let us see if we can get it from your mind."

'All right, I have one.'

"Will you change that name, as it would call him here if you held the thought."

'Would not that be true of others?'

"No. For someone else might be away from your attraction."

'You have spoken of permanent attractions between persons in the spirit world. Are these always between persons of opposite sex?'

"Not necessarily; yet the two of opposite sex belong together. It is said, though I only know from hearsay, that everyone has a mate of the opposite sex, and that at last they come together and form a perfect union of wisdom and love. That does not exclude other very warm ties, however."

'Is there as much difference between the sexes there as here?'

"No. The magnetic attraction is probably the influence. You can feel that to a certain extent in earthly ties, can you not?"

'How about the associations in your circle? Does sex make any difference there?'

"Not much. We are all friends, and when we belong to the same circle it means that we are attracted by the same thoughts, plans, desires, and tastes. Of course this means that we are in tune with each other; there are no jarring notes, the vibrations are the same."

"We are not male and female as on earth. The sex question is one of beauty and naturalness here, quite removed from the coarseness of the earth attraction. It is one of vibration; one of harmony; one of coming together of two forces, like the positive and negative currents of electricity. Yet it exists, and adds to the joy of this life. But it never interferes as it does on earth, with other loves and other companionships. All is within the power of magnetic attraction.

"We wish the heavenly attraction to be understood. It is the great joy of this life, yet so far removed from its earthly phase as to bear small resemblance. Many of the coarser natures that come here are disappointed at first, and it takes a long time to come into the finer qualities of affection. But once they realize it, there is no regret for the loss of their earthly love. Such natures stay on lower planes for a long time. All the higher education is hindered by their attitude and they progress slowly. These too are the material-minded spirits who send over false messages, and who would entangle mortals in their own false teachings. They are a recognized power for evil here, and we often have to protect mortals from them."

An old friend of Sis was introduced by Mary one evening. Speaking of him she said:

"He came here a short time ago full of theories and beliefs of what this life would be; but found himself only an ignorant child, with everything to learn and most of his earthly wisdom to unlearn. He thinks he received a hint or two while still in the earth life that might have educated him if he had followed where they led, but he was too bound by his former convictions. He wishes now to send some word to other teachers, that they may not make the same mistake and waste their energy in teaching unwise doctrines. The world is waking to a definite knowledge of this life and the need of new inspiration to higher and more spiritual ideas."

Then Mary wrote directly for this friend:

"I was spiritually minded, I know; but I confused creed with character. Now I know that character is more than creed, or rather character forms the creed. Character is the inner impulse from the soul and explains itself to the outward brain by principles that really are a creed. But we reversed that in our teaching and many were confused and drifted away."

'What would you say is the foundation of character?'

"The first impulse from the soul should be kindness. One could not go far astray with that as a foundation; then truth and justice."

It seems a common error in thinking of the growth and progress of the spirit world, to conclude that as character grows more perfect personalities grow more nearly alike. I had that idea to some extent when I asked:

'Do spirits retain their personalities as they advance, or do they finally become merged in a state of perfection like Nirvana?'

"Nirvana is a discovery or invention of the eastern, so-called Adepts, and does not exist. Personality goes on and on, otherwise spirits would not have been created with personalities. What is all the discipline of earth for, if not for the development of individual character? No! The individual may go on to unthought-of intelligence, or glory, or perfection; but remains the individual spirit still."

Another writer illustrates this by comparing the progress with an orchestra. The more nearly perfect each instrument and each performer becomes, the more each contributes to the greater perfection of the orchestra as a whole. Unbelievers in spirit communication often strongly criticize conversations or messages purporting to come from persons they had known, claiming they are not like such expressions in the earth life.

An old acquaintance of Sis referred to this as follows:

"I am sure I do not talk as of old, but why should I? 'As of old' would be the orthodoxy of that time. But we are emancipated from all that, and are a part of a life so infinitely fine and so infinitely satisfactory that words can scarcely express it."

After talking with my father one time, I said:

'Your talk does not sound as it used to; but then I don't know that I should expect it.'

"I hope it doesn't; for if it did, then there would have been no advancement. Could anyone but an imbecile be here in the midst of all that is good and beautiful, in the midst of new thought and new activities of mind and body, with the wonders of the universe to attract him, and then after seventeen years of such life and opportunity talk the same as of old? Will you tell me that!"

'I suppose seventeen years there would be the equivalent of a hundred here?'

"Try to drop comparisons, for there are none. Perhaps we might use the old simile, 'as a thousand years to one day,' etc., but all comparisons fail."

In a paper which Sis read at a small gathering she used quotations from matter received from Prof. James. These were criticized by some in the audience as not like his style of writing. Prof. James afterward wrote:

"That may be the case. But at any rate, a change in belief and a change in environment are bound to change the expression."

We receive much instruction regarding the earthly life; and the following is selected in order to show how thought influences character and personality:

"You cannot understand the power of thought—its ability to bring to itself the conditions of its own making. Therefore think wisely, truly, unselfishly; and, above all, spiritually. These are the heavenly impressions that bring us near to you and you near to us.

"I wish to impress this strongly upon your thought if possible. If all could see the building power of thought, little by little, day by day, year by year, they would harbor no evil thought. But they do not see, and therefore have to begin at the beginning here. Think heavenly thoughts and you are drawing near to heaven.

"The thought of earth life is either retarding or advancing the spirit life. Therefore, do you see, that heaven is nearer or farther away according to the thoughts you think."

One's character and personality determine his relationship to his fellow creatures. We have been told several times that the different circles there are builded upon foundations determined by the similarity of tastes, desires, and work; and this has been emphasized in many communications.

We asked regarding the distance between circles and planes, and were told:

"Distance does not mean a great deal here, but congeniality does. We are divided more by sympathies than by distance. The uncongenial never belong to the same circle."

Later we find in our record:

"We love old friends here, but not because they are old. Congeniality is the law of spiritual friendship; and we understand better than formerly in how many ways we can be congenial."

Something had been said about the evils arising from race prejudice on earth, and Mary commented as follows:

"There is no aristocracy of spirit. All meet and associate as their natures desire. The laws of sympathy and congeniality prevail, and there is no color line, of course, to be a barrier."

'Are there any foreigners in your circle?'

"Not as yet. There is no tendency to debar anyone from the circle, but those who are here are grouped together because of similar tastes. We have different homes and different work; but we meet together for interchange of ideas."

And she said at another time when this or an allied subject was discussed:

"It is the law of congeniality that works for happiness here. You know how on earth something is apt to jar when two people come together. You know how difficult it is to be in harmony with the different personalities surrounding you, or making the social life in which you move. Well, all is different here. There is no jarring of souls. We simply know our soul companions and meet them with confidence and love. Others too we meet, but always with only the side turned toward them that is in the same vibration with them. We do not hate; we do not avoid even; but spirit meets its own."

Then the subject of family ties came up when we were asking about a man who had not progressed there, although his family had gone on to higher circles.

'Families do not stay together then?'

"No, not often. Each goes the way he prefers."

'The love of his family was wasted on this man then?'

"Love is never wasted. The influence is always felt. But he does not realize yet the power and beauty of spiritual affection."

'How important are family and relatives to one another?'

"There is not much importance to family ties; more by congeniality."

Another communicator added:

"You are talking of relationships. You are related by the thoughts you think, by the ideas you cherish, by the loves you develop. These are our relationships here, and are dearer and nearer than ties of blood."

Another also wrote: "I have a word to say about family ties too. I have been here long and have found many to love who were in nowise related. Yet for our family I have great tenderness: For one brother here, because he is struggling up through great difficulties; for another, because he is still so far away from real happiness; and for the two brothers who came over in infancy, because of their nobility and purity."

Upon learning that one married couple, whom we had known, were not together there, we asked if many kept together.

"Not many are married in spirit, and it is only in the spirit that the tie continues on this side. Comparatively few keep that tie here, but are happier to each go his own way. They find their mates at last and come into perfect happiness."

The subject of personality and its influence took quite a different turn one evening when, after reading of some wonderful demonstrations in psychometry, we asked to know more about it.

"It is true that character can be impressed upon lifeless objects. The mind of man is infinite in its power, and may influence through touch many inert things. The lava from the volcano, the jewel from a mummy, that you speak of had taken something from the environment and carried it to a sensitive soul. The touch of a hand on an object is much, and in the hand of an intermediate person it may even take something from the mind. Will this help you to understand the influence of mind upon matter?

"You give something of yourself to everything that you touch, and more of yourself to every mind with which you are in contact. This is the source of personal influence, and goes out from you even though you do not so intend. Study the intricacies of mental influence with the object of increasing your power for good."

'What a power evil persons must have in this?'

"Their influence is negative and therefore less powerful. The positive is the power for good."

Still another phase of personal attraction was illustrated when we asked if everyone on earth had a 'guide' in the spirit world.

"Each one there attracts someone here, and such a one is often desirous of helping the one on earth, and becomes what you call a 'guide.' Those on earth receive from teachers here, oftentimes not recognizing the source of the thought given to them; and so in a way they are guided from here."

'It is not necessarily, then, someone who had known the person on earth?'

"Not at all. A matter more of similarity of thought and desire."

This close connection between persons here and those beyond was brought out quite clearly when we asked Dee if she would have known if we had had an accident while riding in the automobile.

"Instantly! A messenger would have called me and I would have been with you. We do not anticipate anything of the kind, and see no warning of it in the outlook for you; but if it did occur we would be notified at once and we would be with you in a flash. There are clairvoyant messengers who are watching and seeing any necessity of calling friends of mortals when such mortals need help."

'Then we are always under the eye of some spirit?'

"Always in the sight of invisible friends! The guardianship by spirit forces is one of the protections thrown around individuals. I do not mean that they can always prevent danger or accident or suffering. But if they cannot do this they are ready with impressions that may help as needed. We get the signal as you might get a telegram. The watchers are ever alert, and call the guides whenever necessary. We have to guard our charges at all times. The watchers are called to this work by the higher powers. It is recognized that this plane needs careful watchers to prevent the evil and destructive forces from exercising their influence. If we call them sentinels, as in the army, you will understand their efficient and necessary work. They are those who seem to be especially fitted for such work—detective service, you might call it—and their signals to us call us immediately."

'Is everyone here so cared for?'

"Yes; that is true even of those who are not in touch with this life. We have to guard the evil as well as the good."

'I should think they might do more in keeping them from evil?'

"You must understand that we cannot use force even in protecting others, and many on earth are so debased that spiritual help could not reach them. Their guards try to protect, but fail because of their earthly and sinful selves. Free will must always be left to assert itself, and the evil on earth will naturally incline towards evil influences from here. You are desirous of good, and therefore good influences reach you. Some walk into wrong paths unintentionally; and because it was not their intention, they are soon brought back."

I asked Mary if some here who learned that they were influenced from there, would not resent any such idea, thinking they alone should have the credit for any advance or good they might experience.

"If that is true, then they will be left to themselves, and will only be helped when they desire the help."

Guardian spirits and heavenly guides suggest the subjects of 'guides' and 'controls,'—terms much used by spiritualists, usually in connection with spirit manifestations or communications.

"A 'control' is only a powerful helper on this side," we were told by Mary. "You might speak of me as a 'control' if you so wished, though I am not a very strong one. Yet I do in a way control the communications of this circle, keeping out, as far as I can, unworthy or ignorant communications, and bringing to you the wise and good. I like the word friend, or instructor better; but many adopt the word 'control.'"

16

VIBRATIONS AND MUSIC

~

WE mortal folk speak easily and confidently of vibrations as if quite understanding their character and power. But what of vibrations whose speed is greater than light, whose rapidity is almost beyond earthly computation? We learn something of such forces from the descriptions of travel and of music in the celestial realm.

"Vibration," we are told, "is the great spirit force here as it is the great material force there; for it is a power affecting both spirit and matter. Scientists stop with earthly vibrations; but why should they? There are numerous evidences of higher ones, if they would accept the evidence."

"The whole system of vibrations is controlled by spirit, for it is one of the forces belonging to spirit movement and power. Everything in this life is more or less connected with vibration, and controlled largely by the individual spirit. Does one wish to travel with speed, he makes use of rapid vibratory action. Does one wish music, then other vibrations are set in motion. Some are produced by individual effort, some are a power used by the individual; just as the different powers are used on earth."

"Have you any conception of what the music of this life may be? Do you ever wonder what it is like? It is caused by vibrations, but produced in the ether by conditions you do not know. They are started by the will of the musician in a manner you cannot understand; but you may know that the thought of the composer may express itself directly without the slow medium of writing, or even of performing. Can you conceive the thought as a material atom, if we may so express it, that moves outward from its producer and goes on its way with influence in proportion to its quality?"

'Do you have mechanical means of reproducing music, or does the author have to send it from his mind each time?'

"We have spirit instruments as we have spirit houses. How else could we get the grand total of harmonious production? Sounds are set vibrating on the spirit instruments according to the conception of the artist or the performer, and the variety of tone or subject is as varied as the thought of the musical mind. Some prefer the quick and joyous tones and chords; others still hold earth's memories in retrospective thought, and their music grows pensive and perhaps pathetic; while others are filled with the desire for intricate harmonies. But all are beautiful, each in its own way.

"Any description of spirit instruments would be beyond your conception. But nothing on earth is so perfect and so beautiful in tone."

'How about the great singers who have been so famous and so loved on earth?'

"The beauty of music and its power of expression does not depend upon the voice, and may carry its message to the heart without song. It may appeal to one with the same power but by different means. We can sing if we wish, though the exquisite effects produced by heavenly instruments make the use of the voice less desired."

'Do you have anything there that is comparable to an orchestra or to an organ?'

"Will you put out of your mind any idea that heavenly music is inferior to that of earth! You do not conceive of spirit power or heavenly music. These are things we cannot make plain to you. But the music you love best is only the slightest indication of that which you may—

"Oh, I get lost for words!"

Sis asked an old school friend who had been a fine pianist on earth if she kept up her music there.

"Not much," was the reply. "It is all so wonderful, I feel myself unable to learn the methods by which it is produced."

'Music was an easy accomplishment for you here.'

"I had the keyboard before me there and could find the combinations easily, it is true. But here! Oh, my dear! If you could only know the difference between earthly and celestial music!

"You are wondering how it is that I, who have been here so much longer than Mary, should not have entered into the study of music before she did. You see, so far as spiritual knowledge was concerned, I was a child when I came over, and had to begin as children do. I could not hear sounds for a long time; spiritual deafness, you might call it. And so I began with other things, and grew so interested that I almost forgot music. Then when my discovery of musical vibrations came I wished to know how they were produced, and went to a teacher of the science. But I did not give enough time to it, because interested in other things; and so Mary got ahead of me. The study is fascinating, as you will learn for yourself when you come. We will perhaps make music together as in the old days. Will not that be fine?"

We were talking of the different specialties in study there, and Sis asked Mary what my study was likely to be.

"Mary thinks he will like history and philosophy, and music too, though he will hardly make music a specialty. Music is very absorbing, and often takes the attention very closely of those who choose it."

I remarked that that would be apt to make them one-sided, as we sometimes found musicians here.

"One-sided? No! Not here! But rounded out and in sympathetic touch with all knowledge."

Then one whom Sis had known as a teacher of music in her girlhood days added:

"One does not have to be absorbed by anyone taste or study here; for days are longer and studies easier than on earth. I am interested in art, philosophy, and many things besides music. Just now I am evolving a new instrument of music, and new harmonies to fit the instrument. I hope to succeed, and when you come you can hear the result."

One evening when we were still discussing vibrations, the pencil wrote:

"Will you care to take a message from one who understands vibrations?"

And then came a message that seemed to be a summing up of the different remarks on the subject that had been given before.

"In the first place put out of your mind all ideas of ordinary movement. For nothing exists in material life so fine, so powerful and so rapid as spirit vibration.

"We use the movement for our work in nearly all ways— in travel, in building, in music, in art, in the very speech of this life. And the study of this force is the most careful and perhaps the most difficult of all. The power depends upon the speed; the speed depends upon the spirit. For the worker must learn to grade and use the force in accordance with law. Nothing is guess work; nothing happens by chance. All is orderly. All can be acquired by study.

"You say this is not definite. Could you describe an unseen and unknown property to one entirely ignorant of that property? To attempt a comparison, Mary has asked if you could describe the fragrance of a rose.

"How about the flavor of a fruit to one who had never known the taste? You can say sweet or sour or bitter; but these convey no meaning to one who has never tasted sweet or sour or bitter. So, you see, we can only give the crudest examples of the effects of certain powers, because we cannot explain the finer meaning.

"I can say then that vibration is our power. We study its properties and its uses. We learn to control. And when we have finally become capable of using it we become workers with infinite resources and power at our command."

Then Mary added:

"This teacher was one who was a scientist on earth, and would have used scientific terms if he could have impressed them on your mind. But as you could not take them he tried to give you more general ideas."

'Are there not mediums through whom you can write any word you wish?'

"I think so, but they are rare. We usually have to fit our language to the ability of the medium. That is why so many mistakes occur, and why messages are mistrusted—because the language is not like that which the communicator used on earth."

17

EVIL

~

THE joys of that life had been for a long time so wonderfully portrayed that we began to wonder if the malicious ones of earth were to be allowed to enter into equal happiness. One evening this thought was answered, even before it was expressed in words.

"You are thinking," the pencil wrote, "that we have not emphasized sufficiently the consequences of an evil life; that we have not warned the selfish and the malicious ones, and have allowed this life to seem too easy of achievement; and we wish to say, every time and all the time, that character is of the first importance.

"As a man lives on earth, so will he appear on this side. Slipping out of the mortal body does not always mean entrance into perfect happiness. Justice, purity, unselfishness, and kindness of heart, are the passports to the heavenly life. If these are lacking they must be acquired, and sometimes the effect of mortal sin makes this acquirement very difficult, and often the time is long and unhappiness great, before the evil is eliminated from the soul. We cannot make this too strong or the caution too serious!

"Selfishness appears to us here as the foundation of all sin. It appears to be the root of all evil, and is insidious in its destruction of character. Selfishness may be only superficial or it may be deeply ingrained in the individual. The first may be overcome when true knowledge takes the place of vanity and superficiality; the second is the foundation of so much evil that it is most debasing in effect, and most difficult to overcome. It masquerades often in fine dress, for many strive for beauty selfishly; make music and art a matter of personal pride; or adorn themselves with exquisite textures and priceless gems; and forget the deeper meaning of spiritual loveliness. The selfish use of wealth and power; lack of sympathy for the poor or suffering; pride; self-esteem—all these, and many other manifestations of self-love, are working toward spiritual atrophy."

'How about those who take their own lives to get rid of the evils of this existence?'

"When a human life is broken by the owner of that life, there is a long period of unconsciousness before any reconstruction can take place. Years may elapse before they are ready to begin any advancement. The suicide takes his own way instead of God's way; and the result is, to paralyze the finer spiritual qualities, and prevent entrance into the joy of this life for a long time."

'Will the world ever come into true Christianity?'

"It will come eventually. Every individual has the power to bring that blessed time a little nearer. The work goes on from here as well as there, and all are needed; for the strife between good and evil grows daily more vicious on the side of evil and needs daily reinforcements on the side of good."

'You believe that final victory will be with the good?'

"I know it will. But there must be greater power both here and there. We see the evil, but not in the hopeless way you see it, for we see also the remedy."

'Does evil persist into the higher planes?'

"No; one leaves all that as one ascends; or, rather, one does not ascend until all evil has been eliminated."

'Can an evil spirit enter into or take possession of a human being?'

"Everyone is free to control his own individuality. We are not allowed to take possession."

'But there are apparent possessions; how about them?'

"Evil spirits break the laws here just as they do there, but there must be a receptive attitude in the individual or no possession would be possible."

'Then the old story of selling one's self to the devil may be approximately true?'

"Yes; many have done this unknowingly."

'Can you tell us the origin of evil?'

"That is not for us to know at present. The origin is so far away in an unknown past that only the Creator of us all can rightly tell of its origin and use. But we know that all things work toward a final greater good, and that is sufficient for us at present."

'Is the percentage of good people any greater now than a hundred years ago?'

"The percentage is far greater than formerly. But the quiet lives of the good, with their unseen and unselfish service, do not get to the knowledge of the public as do the riotous actions of the evil-minded ones."

'Is the world growing better?'

"The good are growing better; the evil are growing more evil still."

One afternoon while Sis was sitting alone and in a passive and receptive mood with hands folded in her lap, her left hand was slowly drawn away. Almost at once her right hand was shaken in the way used by Mary as a signal for writing. So she went to the little table and took up the pencil, which wrote quickly and with great emphasis:

"You are not in the right environment. We cannot see you. Something is clouding you around. What is it?"

'Was it not you moving my left hand?'

"No. Some other spirit was trying to get control. We could not see which one, but came to protect you."

'There is some danger, then, even in the receptive attitude?'

"Evil spirits are here, but help is here also. Just now someone was trying to reach you, and for some reason you were enveloped in a cloud. We think this other influence was trying to conceal you from us."

"You must never lose the consciousness that it is on this plane nearest the earth that good and evil forces first congregate, and the malicious ones may be able to influence receptive minds there. Approach the unseen side of life with reverence, and with desire for spiritual help and knowledge, if you would draw toward you the wise and good of this life."

'Can you influence the evil-minded ones on earth?'

"We are sent to try to lead them into better thought and life. Sometimes the evil ones are open to impressions and we can help. But many times all avenues to the soul are closed and we can find no entrance."

'We have heard of moneymaking schemes, and sometimes of oil, or mine promoting projects, started from that side, victimizing the credulous ones of earth.'

"That is from the evil influences here. Appeals to selfish interest, to money-making, to earthly advancement, to selfish happiness, or selfish projects in any form, cannot be trusted. If only we could convince the world that unselfishness and service for others are the laws of spiritual advancement, all this evil teaching would be of no avail."

We spoke once of the apparent injustice of an all-powerful Ruler allowing so much sin and suffering as the world has witnessed. Mary's reply is worthy of study:

"Human logic fails indeed to explain the infinite purpose of God; the life on this plane seems necessary to prove the wisdom of that purpose and its final beneficence. We do not yet belong to the angelic host where wisdom is proven and mercy apparent; but we know there is a reason for even the cruelties of earth and the sufferings of the innocent."

"We know it is hard to realize the kindness that is intended for man when in the midst of crime, cruelty, and suffering. We here understand it as a forward step in the evolution of character. Man has been given the power of choice. If he chooses wrongly he must learn the wrong by the consequence of his choice."

'But, aside from the real crimes, there are the pleasure-seeking, the vanity, the extravagance of the foolish?'

"What would you have—that they should be compelled into a different course? Can you not see the uses of illness, poverty, and suffering? All these are lessons to lead them into different perceptions of life and its final outcome. They may be the beginnings of wisdom. Many will not learn until they have slipped off the mortal coil. Many will go on, even here, clinging to misleading hopes and pleasures until finally wisdom is born and their true education begins."

A few additional sentences were received later in explanation of the sorrows and tribulations of the human race on earth.

"The human kind moved slowly out of their animal propensities and limitations. The law of 'self-determination' is universal, and is given for the development of character and the final good, which is far better than automatism."

'But the price of choice—of free will—is so terrible?'

"The price is little when compared with the good as we see it here."

'How is the human power of choice better than character foreordained to be perfect?'

"Foreordained character would be automatism, and would eliminate personality, individuality, and would result in weariness and monotony."

Sis spoke of the flaunting headlines in the daily papers—of murder, dishonesty, and all manner of crime, and the comparatively small space given to the recital of good deeds.

"True wisdom and virtue do not advertise themselves. What do you know of the secret thoughts of the wise and good, and the plans that are crystallizing for the betterment of the world?"

'But perhaps you do not see the evil here as we see it?'

"We see the aura surrounding evil lives, and the misery that follows. Wicked ones are here—murderers and their victims, thieves, robbers, the vile and the cruel, the selfish and the unjust.

"The work of this circle is not with the wicked ones here, though we are asked to use our influence toward purer thought and nobler living. And although our lives are filled with joyous service for the most part, we are also glad to help in this other sphere of work."

'How can you be so happy when there is so much evil over there?'

"The evil ones are not near us as a rule. We may go to them to help them, and we are sometimes obliged to neutralize their mischievous influence. But these are not frequent occasions. Our work is of a different sort. There are many who are engaged in this work, for many have the missionary spirit as on earth. And these are the ones who go to the undeveloped or the wicked, and strive to bring them into higher living. And their work is not in vain."

'Do these evil ones have much influence on better spirits?'

"That is to be guarded against; but there are circles among the lower orders as among the higher ones. Each goes to 'his own place.' That is where his congeniality is expressed—to those of his own thought and purpose. They do not influence each other downward as much as you might think. They generally seek their own, and having found their own, they remain until uplifted by some finer influence. They usually rise nearly in a company. A thought or influence affecting one, is apt to affect the circle, and because of this it is easier to lead them."

18

UNDEVELOPED SPIRITS

~

IT is customary in this life to spend many of our earlier years in education in preparation for the years to follow. Most people, however, seem to proceed as though the eternal life beyond, if there is such a thing, would have to take care of itself. If any preparation is necessary, there is time enough to do it in the afterlife, they seem to argue. There is time enough, of course; and we learn that very many have to go through the preparatory course after arriving on the other side. If this were all, the matter might not be quite so important. But we also learn that it is not necessary to waste these first years there in that manner, if certain things are done in the earth life, and certain other things avoided. The education, if acquired in this life, is short and easy, and, moreover, is a great aid to a successful life here. It consists of following as nearly as is practical the teachings and the example of Christ—just the life that we as Christians are supposed to follow.

But evidence from the life beyond indicates that many, very many, either through ignorance or through willfulness, have not been as successful in carrying out Christ's teachings as they might have been, and as they would try to be, I am sure, if a knowledge of the consequences was thoroughly known. We have learned that this education, when left for the afterlife, is too often complicated by the results of unkind deeds and thoughts in this life; and also by having to unlearn many things that have been wrongly learned or understood while here.

This last is a handicap little thought of by those who have not investigated. It is frequently a serious one. It has been brought to our notice very strongly in various ways. The following is one instance:

"I am not trying for marvels or wonders, but I do want to try to give a plain, simple statement of the life here that may lead some anxious, fearing soul into more faith and happiness. I wish I could save them from looking forward with fear into the dark unknown. Will you try and take what you can, and I will try and write what I can, of comforting thought to all those who are really trying to live the right life on earth, and desiring a new inspiration for the future.

"Many come so very ignorant, and come into such a long sleep and unconscious period, which we are sure is unnecessary, for they have not believed the truth of active spiritual development here. So they lose time, and lose the power at first of realizing the life and all it means.

"Tell all who come in the circle of your influence that they are making their future now, and can almost control this future condition, if they will only seek the truth and abide in it while still on earth.

"I do not often preach, but feel like a sermon tonight.

"For the souls that come to this side come in such multitudes that they can scarcely be counted, yet only here and there are the spiritually developed ones, the ones who can enter into this life with joy, and commence the development of spiritual power at once. The pity of it gets hold of us here, now and then, and we feel like trying to bombard the earth with spirit bombs—something to make the people think, something to force them away from their material thoughts, pleasures, and plans.

"We are obliged to begin our work with them as we would begin with children, and not even in that way when they first come. They sink into a state that is hard to be described. They are not even ready to think. Brain and sense and heart and soul have so long been educated wrongly that silence and unconsciousness are the only remedies at first. Then there comes a confused awakening, with all their human habits of thought and all their evil selfishness predominant. What can be done, then, except to put strong forces in control, that they at least may be kept from harming others. You cannot conceive of this work, I am sure; but it is very real here."

'But you do not do this—you with all your dainty, fairy children to teach?'

"No, but I watch others in the patient, self-controlled effort, and I realize how strong must be their faith and hope, to continue in the work. They do succeed at last, but it is often a long and weary way; and but for the strong, bright and enduring faith of such workers and teachers, it would be almost unendurable."

'Such are kept separate, are they not? They do not mingle with you?'

"Yes, surely. Each 'goes to his own place,' as the Bible says. But we can watch the work of transformation, and we can give to the workers our own best thoughts and encouragement. That is our part of it."

We said we had thought of this phase there and had spoken of it.

"It exists, and is one of the great opportunities for work for the great and blessed spirits who undertake it.

"I have preached a sermon this time; but it may be well for you to know of the darker shadows over here.

"But we are also blessed with the sight of the brave spirits who are working with the low and debased ones of earth, and were filled with the pity of it; the unnecessary waste of lives there and the unnecessary waste of time here in bringing them into spirit lives. Then, too, all these brave teachers who give themselves to this work, might be released for other and pleasanter work, if only—if only, the earth people knew the truth."

A specific instance of the slow development that can occur there will be given now, and it is a pleasure to think that we may have assisted a little in his progress.

In earlier years Sis had a friend whom she knew very well; they were young people together. This young man, whom I will call Frank Chase, was a man of high ideals concerning this life, but very positive in his beliefs. He held in ridicule all ideas of communication with the unseen world, if indeed he held a belief that there was such a world. His interest was most keen in the mechanics and scientific discoveries of the day. He passed over in early manhood.

Sis had inquired concerning him several times, but received little information beyond the statement that he had not advanced very far, which she thought very surprising. Some months ago we were asked quite unexpectedly:

"Will you send a message to Frank Chase? If you did he might like to come to this circle. If we can interest him in this work it will be well for him.

"He seems to question everything, and doubts even the spiritual life. He knows, of course, that he has passed away from earth, but is busy explaining that and many other things, with a philosophy of his own. He has a bright brain and we wish to turn it to the truth, and lead him into the real life here. That is why I asked you to send him a message. He does not know you are communicating. We believe that if he can find himself—that is, realize that he is a spirit and living a spirit life already, that he will begin to study and grow."

The next day the pencil wrote:

"After talking with you yesterday, I turned, and with the quickness of thought, was far away; so far that it would have taken you days to accomplish the journey.

"We went to see the one to whom we wish you to speak, and we have brought him to our circle to talk to you. He does not believe it can be done. Can you convince him? Will you speak to him?"

Sis said:

'Well, Frank Chase, are you really here to talk to me again after all these years?'

Mary said:

"He does not believe it is you. Call to his mind someone he used to know."

Sis complied by asking:

'Do you remember going to New York to see a young lady?'

"Will you tell him how she looked?"

Sis gave a short description of the young lady, and Mary said:

"Will you keep on. He is impressed."

Sis asked if he remembered this young lady coming to where he lived.

"Keep right on. He is interested."

After further talk we were told:

"He knows now it is you, and is overjoyed to know it is possible to talk with and hear from earth, which he has never done before."

After some further conversation Mary said:

"He is so surprised that he can hardly credit it at all. Yet he knows that only you could tell him some of these things. We will bring him again soon; it is a good beginning. He is startled, and can hardly believe; but will probably wish to investigate, as that is his turn of mind, and that is what we wish."

We asked if they could explain how he had been getting along all these years without learning more.

"Try to think of yourself in a dream, a long dream, and everything happening in ways that are strange, yet you do not wonder about it. Your dream accepts the things as true. That is as near as I can describe his situation. When he first came, he was met by his father and sister, but they failed to reach his reasoning mind and he has wandered on in this condition through all these years."

At another time he came of his own accord to Mary, wishing to talk. After a short conversation Sis asked if in all that time he had been there he had heard of the many wonderful inventions that had appeared here in the meantime. He had not, and wished to know about them. First was the telegraph. Yes, he remembered that. But the telephone was new, and the wireless, and automobiles. Then we went on to tell of the great war, and the immense ships that carried our soldiers, and the terrible guns, and the liquid fire.

He had heard a little of the war, but did not believe it possible to do such things.

"What are the good things of earth?" he asked.

This came near being a 'poser', but Sis spoke of the Red Cross work, the hospitals, the aid to the starving, etc. Mary said:

"He thinks the world must be in a terrible condition with so much science producing evil things. Tell him of the great vessel that was sunk by the Germans. Tell him about the ship that was sunk by an iceberg."

We talked some time, and after some remark of Sis, he said:

"What am I going to hear from you next! No one else could have told me the things you have. I did not know it could be done."

Mary added:

"He is dazed with the thought, but he will take it to think over as he did the last time. You are certainly getting hold of him and we must keep it up."

'This is startling, Mary! How can such things be?'

"Will you believe that each one makes his own life; each one has the chance and must develop accordingly.

"Frank Chase's condition was caused by too much doubt, too much unbelief in a spirit life. He would not believe he was in a heavenly sphere, and would not admit that he needed help; but argued himself into a strange and persistent unbelief, until the desire for anything different almost disappeared."

The next time he came, Mary wrote for him as follows:

"I am here. Your teacher will write for me. I have been so unbelieving that I could get nothing, of course; and so I had no proof of the connection between the two worlds. But what you have said convinced me, and I am studying now so that I too can get in touch with mortal lives."

Mary added:

"There have been years, he says, when he believed he was on some plane above the earth, but did not understand that this plane might be the beginning of heavenly life for him. It is hard to make you understand, and he says now it is hard for him to understand; and it seems to him more like a long, long dream than anything else he can compare it to. He is learning fast, and is far happier than before, and pursues his studies eagerly."

This was an amazing experience for us. We had read something of such things, but it was all so strange we had passed it by. But this brought the truth to our realization with much force.

It seems these unfortunate spirits can frequently be helped from this side quicker than from there, if they can reach someone whom they knew. But they eventually find the way out of the fog in some manner, in any case; though as we were told, it may be years and years. Such spirits have not necessarily led evil lives while here. More often this spiritual handicap is the result of too strong belief in some superstition, some creed, or some philosophy on earth; a case of being certain that one way is right and all others wrong.

Such beliefs and philosophies continue with them more or less strongly on the other side, just as superstitions sometimes cling to one here in spite of all the evidence there may be to show they are without foundation.

That a development complete enough to enable one to advance to higher planes may be delayed almost indefinitely, is revealed by an incident given us recently. I will give it just as it appears on our records:

In looking over our records there will be found a number of instances when Mary has said that Sis was surrounded by a cloud. Several times she has said she thought this cloud was the result of some other power trying to manifest through the pencil. In these cases very little has been written; and numerous times when Sis has been alone, not a movement occurred.

Early this afternoon she could get nothing. A little later, when I was present, only a few words came through. Late in the afternoon, however, Sis tried to get passive when alone, and her hand began to shake, showing that someone wished to write. Mary then wrote freely and gave an explanation of the perplexing troubles.

Sis was trying to get in communication with Mary because of a letter I had received from a friend. It seems that this friend had been to a psychic who had given a message for Sis. This message was as follows:

"There is an ancient spirit way back in the times of Mahomet, who says he has been trying to reach Miss D, and says he has something of importance to say to her, and begs you to give a message which he wants to send. He wants her to write as a heading on her paper, 'The Seers and Sages of the Present Day,' and then wait in silence for his message."

When Mary finally succeeded in writing, the following was received:

"We are here, and you were led by us. Do not doubt.

"We could not give that other one the opportunity. He would have misguided you."

'Was it the 'ancient spirit' we were told to expect?'

"Yes, he is an ancient force or teacher, but is not of the kind we trust. He has not learned the real truth in the ages he has lived. He would teach you of occult mysteries as they existed in the olden time. We do not wish the unseen to be represented by mysteries, rites, and observances. Remember we belong to an age in which the teachings of Christ have purified religious belief; and we, in the unseen, strive to make his teachings still powerful on earth. We do not know just what that other message would have been, but we do know that you, as well as we, wish for the truth as Christ gave it to the world. Are you satisfied?"

'Yes, that is what we wish.'

"We try to guard you always from such influences, and it is because we do this that at times you do not even get us. We cannot come through an influence so strong that it takes our force to neutralize it.

"You trust us and that is well. Keep with us as long as we teach the truth that Christ taught on earth—humility, unselfishness, the love of humanity, and the striving to make the world better."

Sis inquired of the reliability of any of the ancient sages or rulers who wrote through others.

"We do not know any of the ancient kings or princes. We cannot describe or even see them. But this teacher who wished to control your pencil has been here before, and we have checked his influence; and, as he said, he could not get a message to you. Are you sorry?"

'No. We wish your guidance and protection.'

"You are safe while you keep that attitude. The world is likely to go astray if led by those who teach strange rites and occult practices of long ago. Christ, and the truth as made known by Christ, are what we wish to bring to the world. You are safe in such truth and such teaching."

'Was it because you were trying to prevent other powers from sending messages, that I so many times have been unable to write?'

"Yes. We often have all our power taken in simply neutralizing other influences. Remember only mind or spirit force can be used, and if used in preventing other influences it cannot at the same time be used in giving out messages."

'Why did you not tell me what the trouble was at the time?'

"We do not like to admit the power at the time. Be satisfied. We are protecting you always. Good-by now."

Soon after this I came in, and after hearing what had been written, I said:

'Well, Mary, we are very thankful to you.'

"You may well be, for it means your protection and your determination to receive only the truth."

Then to Sis:

"Do you see why we wish you to be our medium even if you have less psychic power than some others?"

I said it was astonishing how many were slow in developing, and how long they were in seeing the truth.

"Can you see how very long people or spirits may be fascinated with their own beliefs? They are so unwilling to be convinced! No wonder that Christ taught the people that they must become as little children!

"We can tell you that many times we have neutralized powerful forces that were untruthful and malicious.

"We are constantly on guard lest some unworthy power succeeds in getting a message to you. We believe you would recognize it usually, but some spirits are subtle, and give sophistries in language that would conceal the malicious influence."

'Mary, just why has nothing been said of this before? Were you afraid we would not understand?'

"Mary does not like to speak of the evil here. It unsettles some earthly minds in their previous beliefs of a heaven of perfection, and we prefer to use constructive rather than destructive influence."

19

PROGRESS

~

THAT all knowledge is at once available to the spirit that continues after death is an idea that has had very general acceptance in the past among the believers in an immortal life. This illogical conception was mentioned in an early chapter together with the more reasonable view of the continuance of development and progress on that side. The slow upward climb of the spirit while it occupies the material frame, and the opportunities for advancement and the delights of accomplishment when this spirit enters upon the new day of its existence, are all so well depicted in the quotations following, that no added comment is thought necessary.

"Wherever there is life there is spirit. The development upward is a matter of time, and again time and again time, before the physical becomes aware of its spiritual powers. Think how long the earth people have been creeping upward, and think how low the attainment is now, and how time and time and time again must elapse before the world becomes entirely spiritualized!

"Study the law of evolution, and watch the progress of the human body from its first inception of material life, coming up through various and innumerable transitions, always from the lower to the higher, and you will have a parallel for the spirit evolution which goes on from here. By evolution I mean progress, growth, and ever increasing perception. You may thus form an idea of the varying life of the spirit; and may, perhaps, guess the joy that comes from its unfoldment. Life here is still progressing to higher forms, and will finally reach a perfection as yet undreamed of by us of this lower plane. What this life can contain of knowledge, wisdom, and joy, is only faintly imagined even by us."

"I have said that life is progression. Now, what is progression? First of all, knowledge,—that is, after character has been established. First, knowledge of the earth from which we here all come; knowledge of the conditions there, and the ways of improving those conditions. For you must know that man would still be the savage, the cave-dweller, or the nomad, if there had been no inspiration from here. Then, knowledge of higher spiritual conditions and the powers that this knowledge gives; knowledge to be used for other lives, sometimes on earth, sometimes on other planets. After this, still increasing knowledge and still increasing power for good. Always giving out; do not forget that knowledge is to be used for others. And so life goes on and service goes on. Eternity is a constantly increasing growth, and a constantly increasing gift to others."

'You speak of man rising from the cave-dweller by inspiration from the spirit world. Has man no initiative of his own to rise to better things?'

"Yes, but it takes many generations to reach the wisdom even of today. If man is left to the slow progress of evolution the people of earth would suffer far longer the mistakes of ignorance and selfishness. There is an upward tendency which in long cycles will bring man to wisdom and righteousness; but we here are glad to turn ahead the clock of time a little."

'It would seem that if this influence is used to any extent, we would see more evidence of it?'

"You do not comprehend the centuries of growth that lie behind you. You think of the ignorant, the low, and the wicked, but do not comprehend that these are lives that are in the process of evolution, and have not yet attained what many other earth lives have achieved. For evolution has not been one grand sweep of the entire human family, but has gone on by degrees and in places, some attaining much while others are almost at the beginning; some almost spiritualized, others scarcely beyond their animal ancestry. Be patient with the low and material ones, and pity rather than blame them."

'There are prophecies of a wonderful wave of spiritualization—that someone will arise to save us from the evils of materialism and selfishness into which we seem drifting. Is there any truth in this?'

"The world moves slowly and no miracle is likely to happen. But if you will just study the past and go back far enough, you will see that the tendency is always upward. But whether the tendency can be measured by years or by centuries, is something which we do not know. The optimists will believe the change will come soon; but the pessimists believe it will be long delayed if it come at all. We can watch and help as best we can, and then wait; and that is what the world will have to do. Our teachers do not tell us of any coming marvel. Just patient effort, and working for the good at all times, is what we are taught as our part of it."

And the final goal seems as indefinite:

"The Creator of all things holds the bounds of life within his power, but we do not know what this highest of all powers allows in the infinite production of life and things. We are moving onward and upward constantly. We can only indistinctly vision what is before us, and our teachers from higher planes have limits beyond which at present they neither see nor know. Can you not see how this stimulates thought and interest? The future lies before us like a great, beautiful, unknown land; and we only step along its borders and look eagerly forward. Curiosity and the desire to know keep us constantly in motion. Motion is life in the material world, and motion is life in thought and in the spiritual world."

"We are trying to tell you a little of this life as it progresses in knowledge, but we have to leave much for your minds to puzzle over, because we have no synonyms for the various work. We have much that would be of interest to you if we could bring it to your understanding. But spirit activity and mortal activity are so utterly different, it is hard to express them in the same terms. We receive much information of the work of those far above us, and this is an inspiration to us in our own study and work. For instance, these teachers have taught us much of the properties of heat and light and electricity, and their multiple uses and powers. You think the scientists there are experts in such things; but they are only at the beginning of knowledge. On the higher planes thought has gone forward into new processes and new forms of activity. These are ever increasing. Just as man has evolved from the cave-dweller with no implements but his hands, to a powerful being who can navigate the sea and air, and surround himself with incomparable luxuries; so the spirit goes on from great to greater, from wise to wiser, and in all the eternities before us we see no end to wisdom, or activity, or the pursuit of enlightenment."

"There are many problems at present hidden even from the higher planes. Study and discovery are among the delights here. There is an infinite amount of undiscovered science still before us. We follow the thought of others, and advance step by step, inch by inch, and are held in wonder and awe at the dim visions before us of the powers and forces yet to be used. We are children yet in the infinite knowledge, and we of mortal birth move along in smaller circles than the spirits of other planes or universes. But can you conceive a little of the joy of acquiring the knowledge that leads us into such limitless wonders! Knowledge is growth, and growth is happiness; and all avenues of thought lead upward to infinite wisdom, justice, and love."

"We are individuals, but we belong in a great scheme of higher consciousness toward which we are all tending. That is the real joy of this life: that it is evolutionary onward and upward to infinite results of which we yet have no complete conception; only dimly perceiving the ultimate joy, wisdom, and affection."

We spoke once of the delights they had mentioned on their plane, and expressed our wonder by remarking that it seemed too good to leave for another.

"You will not be obliged to change until you wish to do so. But neither do you need to dread the higher spheres. As a child you would probably have dreaded the high school, though later you longed for it. And that is the way it is here. Progress is natural, following the development of the mind."

"Many prefer to stay here. We find abundant opportunities for service. We are attracted to the planet we came from and prefer to stay near it for a time. All go on some time, but the time of the change is indefinite and is decided by each individual for himself— at least after a certain degree of advancement is made."

We were talking about progress and evolution in connection with a lecture we had attended. Prof. James added this to the conversation through the pencil:

"The beginning is a long way off from observation and the steps upward are beyond human sight. It is theoretical, but not capable of proof. That which can be proved is from the lower orders leading up to man and onward to eternal life. The altruistic sentiment began in the lower stages, with the parental love first, then love of friend, and home, and country. Then comes the higher development, always, it is true, being more or less mixed with self-hood. But the start is made, and keeps on until the perfection is reached in the love of man and the brotherhood of nations, and that 'far-off divine event' leading upward to godliness and perfect love. It is this that is the need of the world. It is this that should be emphasized—the good of all rather than the advancement of the individual. We here are earnest beyond expression, because we see this need of the world—to emphasize the true life, the life which there may be the beginning of here!

"The 'missing link' that is of the most importance is the brotherhood of man. To us it seems of the first and only importance. The links of the long chain binding man to animal below and to spirit above matter not so much as the perfection and the drawing power of this end of the chain."

In our various metaphysical speculations we spoke one evening of having no knowledge of a beginning, of an end, or of a purpose.

"You might say the same of us here. But the eternal riddle is more nearly answered with us, for we have evidence that the people of the earth do not have.

"Would you like to have all eternity spread out before you like an open book, with nothing more to hope for or evolve? Is it not infinitely more interesting to grow and increase in knowledge, and yet have things far beyond you beckoning to new endeavor and wider knowledge? What would eternity be like if we could absorb its mysteries in one grand sweep of eye or brain? Is it not better as it is?"

'No doubt it is better. But some intelligences somewhere must have acquired all knowledge, for there has supposedly been an infinity of time in which to acquire it?'

But Mary was not to be cornered by any such speculation.

"Well, if this is true, it is all the more interesting, because we may someday come into recognition and acquaintance with the wonderful spirits who have absorbed so much of heavenly knowledge."

'But if perfection has been reached somewhere in this infinity of time, what is that but Nirvana?'

"You carry your imagination too far. There is no limit we are told. The story of creation is not finished. As we all grow toward the light, these future creations will continue."

"You are asking too far-reaching questions. We are both getting beyond our depth. Don't you see what I have told you so many times, that we do not come into all knowledge at once? It is the selection of our study, and it is perseverance in learning that count. We do not try to take up all things at once. We have been here long, many of us, but have scarcely mastered anyone, two, or three of the arts of this life."

'Possibly we are asking questions we should not? Possibly we should work out the answers ourselves?'

"No, you may ask, and we will answer when we can. But we do not know it all, and are willing to tell you when our knowledge fails."

But the big subjects still had attraction for us, and not long afterward we were asking about the creation of the universe.

"Creation is a big subject—too big for us at present. The only thing we can say now is, that out of the existing conditions the earth, the planets, the whole universe was formed; formed according to existing laws. But from what time and what cause proceeded those laws we cannot clearly explain. Remember we are novices yet in spirit understanding. There is an eternity before us in which to learn. Why try to rush past the intermediate spheres of knowledge and reach for something which is at present beyond our comprehension? We here are also subject to immutable law. But within that law lies our liberty, which is so great we do not ask for more.

"Mary is no theologian, and we have need for faith even here. These things are still a mystery, although we believe in the far-off final good that shall come even to the earth. We are not responsible for the earth; we cannot explain the miseries of its life. But we know that compensation exists on this side, and that beyond us undoubtedly lies the explanation which is already reached by wiser minds than ours. 'Shall we talk of something else? We are getting beyond our depth.'"

But again we came back with a big question at another time.

'Is it irreverent to ask if God is a growing, a progressive ruler? Some thinkers here believe that.'

"Mary says: We do not know. But we cannot see why it is not reasonable for the Great Spirit of All to develop more and more, following the law of progress which we see in all who have spirit life. We are glad to perceive the knowledge here; so glad to be a part of the growth; so infinitely satisfied to be moving onward and upward as we increase in learning and in power of discernment, that we can hardly understand the dissatisfaction over the lack of knowledge there; or perhaps we might call it the dissatisfaction caused by the unbelief in divine truth and eternal progress. You are living in a time that tests the souls of mankind. But many are responding to the tests with increased power, wisdom, and love. Is it not worth the price, if, out of this time of trial, higher truth, nobler effort, and spiritual attainment are born? We see it so from this side and are eagerly trying to help the cause of truth and unselfishness and brotherly love in the world. The limit of the human mind is the beginning of the spirit mind, and the people will find it so someday. Be patient with the human mind and its human doubts. Even doubt is better than indifference; for through doubt people think and question, and are on the way to truth."

We were talking with friends one day on various philosophical subjects, and among other things, the position of the Supreme Ruler of the universe; whether he was apart from it as a director, or was in it and in nature stimulating its advance. We inquired through the pencil that evening and were told:

"We will try and answer what we believe to be the truth.

"God is! He has wisdom, intelligence, beneficence, and is above all, in all, and through all, in his knowledge and wisdom, but not in his personal presence. Will you accept the belief as we are trying to give it; for modern philosophy is creating a godless world, and that means a backward movement in all that is highest and best. We do not know God even here by sight or touch; but the power and the wisdom that come to us, most certainly come from an intelligence and power infinitely beyond our own, and we here look to this superior wisdom and benevolence and call it God, the Father of us all."

'Do all who have advanced beyond earthly attractions there believe as you do?'

"Yes, all here who have come into the spiritual conception and knowledge and experience of this life believe as we do, except that as they develop more and more their faith and their reverence grow into higher forms."

'If a person here who had a firm belief in God, but conceived of him as John Burroughs did, for instance—if such a person should be a psychic and be receiving communications as we are, would his teacher tell him the same things you are telling us? What I am trying to get at is: is this the general truth on that side, or do we attract teachers whose opinions largely coincide with our own?'

"Wait a little, we wish someone else to come."

Then after a moment:

"Wm. James is here and says:"

"Such a man would probably attract those whose thought was not antagonistic to his own. I do not mean that there are those here who deny that God exists, but that in their larger ideas of the First Great Cause they would lead him into the true thought by such arguments as would make him feel the harmony of our belief and faith. I could tell such a person all the bypaths and wanderings of my own faith and its final adjustment to the reality as I am conscious of it here. It might be an example of the different trends of human thought and its final acceptance of the truth in the light of this life, in the illumination which the spirit receives when once its earthly shackles have been removed. I was never at rest in my belief, and worked out many logical byways for human intelligence; but when I came over these were forgotten. The truth is supreme; and when once here, all earthly arguments fall away. We here believe in an infinitely wise and great power incarnated in some spirit form finer and different from ours, yet in a way corresponding to our own. We may come into some understanding later which will alter that belief somewhat, but not, we believe, to any vital extent. We look to Christ as our elder brother, and he is far higher than we in wisdom; yet he looks above and beyond to the Infinite Spirit whom he calls Father. Can we do better than to follow his example?"

Finally Mary tried to give us a lesson in another way, to teach us not to be in a hurry to learn everything.

Dee started it by introducing a visitor who she said wished to talk a little. They wrote for him:

"I was a dreamer on earth and wondered about the unseen and unknown. When I came over here the mysteries seemed greater than I had ever dreamed; and many of them are still unexplained to my mind. One of these is the vastness of the heavens and the limitless greatness of the Creator of all things. I cannot yet conceive of the infinite, either in space, time or existence, and I wander through the heavens looking for something to explain these things, something to anchor my belief. Mary says that this is not necessary; that if I will move on patiently and normally, knowledge, understanding, and the power of belief will come. I think she wishes me to write this because you are attempting to reach out for infinite knowledge and understanding when you should rest in faith and hope, and wait for the illumination which she says will surely come when you are ready for it. She says we do not begin to climb from the top of the ladder. We place our feet firmly on the lower round before we begin the ascent, and one by one the rounds will carry us upward, and we will ascend almost without effort.

"That is her theory, and I guess it is a good one."

"Mary says: His words indicate a truth, and I think it a good piece of advice for you. Don't you?"

'Has he gone?'

139

"Yes, he has wandered off again. He is a young man and eager to learn, and will grow faster than he believes. He has not been on this side long."

'Mary, I believe you were 'putting up a job' on us. I don't believe there was a man!'

Mary replied very emphatically:

"Will you know that he is a person, and he did drop in about the time I heard you talking about the many mysteries of life. I did 'put up a job' on you, when I found he had been taking the same way with rather unsatisfactory results, and he seemed to guess that he was my mouthpiece. But what difference does that make? You got the advice all the same."

'But how would we ever find out anything about these great problems if we did not ask questions?'

"That is all right unless it makes you unhappy, or interferes in your belief in the wisdom and goodness of God; in which case it would be a serious obstacle."

'The only evidence of that goodness that seems positive here is the general tendency upward that is shown throughout earth's history.'

"That is one of the proofs of the spirit of God manifesting itself upon the earth. Yet, the very fact of allowing human nature to try its own experiments may also be a proof of his presence. For how can you tell what is designed even in seeming ill? There is a plan, never doubt that, for the final perfection of human life. The suffering will not last forever, and through that suffering good may come— will surely come, we believe. Character, self-control, wisdom, overcoming evil with good, the power of choice, free will: Are not these worth suffering for? Would you be an automaton instead of a thinking being, capable of choice and capable of choosing the right to an eternity of knowledge and growth?"

20

CIRCLES AND PLANES

~

ENTHUSIASTS in all branches of learning or investigation often use words in their writings and descriptions that pertain almost exclusively to their special work. These may be words in common use which have acquired new meanings, or they may be words coined for more specific description. Spirit communication has its share of such words, and some of them have been used so long and so freely that hardly anyone needs a definition of them— such as 'medium,' 'guide,' 'control,' 'plane,' 'aura,' and 'astral.'

Of these the word 'plane' is perhaps the most frequent in our records. We have always wanted to know the 'what,' the 'why' and the 'wherefore' of all these things, and it was not long until we were inquiring about the 'seventh plane,' the 'twentieth plane,' etc., and how they differed one from another. We were told:

"The astral plane is the one nearest the earth. Beyond this are the great outlying spaces and the innumerable higher planes to which the spirits may ascend when prepared, and when they desire to go."

'What constitutes a 'higher plane?'

"I think you will understand it better as a sort of higher grade, like college after high school. It is a different plane or sphere or space where those of a certain degree of advancement can remain for a time.

"These spheres or planes are separated more by spiritual advancement than by distance, though the latter is sometimes great. We ascend as we grow, or we remain to teach others. But it is all normal, and like the different grades of advancement in college or school, if I may use the comparison. Each grade has its peculiar work or degree of advancement, not set by any rule except that of congeniality."

Mary brought another teacher one day, and after he had given his message we asked:

'Do you come from a higher plane?'

"I do not call it a higher, I call it a different plane. There are higher planes, and there are different circles on the same plane. The latter would better express my place. It is not as easy to progress as you may imagine. We have to study for advancement as students there study for the higher grades. We can choose any circle on any plane on which we dwell and remain there as long as we wish."

'Someone has said that thirty years was the longest time spent on one plane?'

"'Someone' was wrong, as a great many 'someones' are wrong, when trying to describe the spirit world.

"We use plane to express groups or circles interested in the same kind of work, and we use it also to express a higher sphere. We can all stay as long as we wish in any circle, or any plane, or any sphere."

'Are these planes separated so that one could speak of them as first, second, third, etc.?'

"No, not that, any more than you could express with mathematical exactness the state of a man's soul. It is all in the progress, and some move upward in one way and some in another. Try to think of spiritual progress in other terms than distance."

Mary made this a little more clear one evening when she said:

"We are on the plane nearest the earth, and are more nearly in touch with human lives than the higher ones.

We love our work here and can stay as long as we wish; or we can go to a higher plane and take up new work and new studies. But in going on we would lose our closeness to those we love, and who have not yet come over. And so we stay and wait and work and love, and try to win our earth friends into happier thoughts of life and death, as you call them; of life and progression as we call them. I had no one especially whom I loved or whom I could help; but you must remember that I came over ignorant of all that pertained to this life, and so I became interested in my work. We will go higher of course, some time, but we will have joy and companionship and work that will be congenial wherever we go."

'Where is 'up,' or 'higher'?'

"That is a hard question for us to answer, because it is an expression of spirit rather than of space. The higher spirits are the ones who have progressed to greater knowledge and acquisition in all ways, and we use the expression 'higher' to convey that meaning to you. They do not occupy the same plane that we do. You may call it 'out' in space, or 'up,' as you choose; for it is a condition rather than a position. Yet they occupy a different position in the great surrounding space, and they are more etherealized, and would not easily come to the denser atmosphere of this lower plane."

In answer to a similar question at another time, Mary said:

"The earthly heaven has no limit so far as we can see. The plane we are on encircles the earth in a broad band of ether that you would think limitless. But we know that there are other planes and other circles. They may extend beyond this universe, taking in all the other planets, so far as I know. I only know that we are in limitless space, and that other circles or planes are in limitless space beyond. By limitless space I mean, of course, limitless as far as our perceptions are concerned. There are limits, perhaps; but we do not see or feel them. Heaven is big enough for all. You will never be crowded."

Many teachers have come to us from higher planes, brought by Mary to tell us about life and conditions, in answer to our questions. One of these teachers said:

"We wish to tell you of the life of the spirit as it progresses from plane to plane. For the grades of spiritual evolution are infinite in number. We will begin with life on the plane next above our own, where higher science is taught, and where many are trying to find answers to problems that confront intelligence there. Life on other planets, with their varying conditions, is one of these problems.

"You do not know the laws of life on the more ethereal planes. You do not know the teachings nor the occupations, and it is these that we wish to bring to you. We will begin with the ethics of the higher life."

'Would they not still be love and service?'

"Yes, but love and service are expressed by different activities. Life on the higher plane is like this, only more spiritualized; just as this plane is like earth life only more ethereal. The higher plane expresses love and service still, but in higher degree and in more spiritualized activities. These activities may extend to other planets or to other universes. We go to higher planes when we choose, and we go to other planes below us to teach them these higher truths, if they wish. All sciences are taught here:—history, chemistry, astronomy, mathematics, biology, and many sciences that the earth has no knowledge of as yet.

"I belong to a higher plane, but I can move to those still higher in pursuit of knowledge, and return to my own plane to teach that knowledge. We are more free as we ascend, and visit many planes far higher than the one we especially inhabit and call our home. But at first, the earthborn mortals would only be confused, like a stranger in a strange city with unaccustomed manners and habits. The freedom of moving to other planes is therefore confined to those already advanced."

Mary said one evening:

"We are told that the higher spirits believe that they have knowledge that the world needs, and like the rest of us, are trying to give it. But life and love are the same in all spheres, and unless they can tell something of their occupations and knowledge acquired on those planes, they are teaching what we who have become versed in the life here are all trying to give: Service, love, knowledge, growth. These are the foundations of all our teaching."

'You communicate much by thought impressions. How far away can these impressions be made?'

"The higher planes use different symbols, different expressions, and messengers who come to us must learn those expressions and interpret to us, like an interpreter of foreign languages, perhaps.

Distance is not so much a barrier as the difference in occupation, thought, and expression. We might impress one in our vibration thousands of miles away, yet might fail to convey our message to one near us."

In the chapter on Messengers I have mentioned the fact that many mediums claim to have teachers from past ages. If these ancient sages have really advanced to a realization of spiritual truth, and really do send their wisdom to earth, it would seem that they are hardly in direct touch with the receiver here, if the following is correct:

"Will you try to take a message from another teacher? He is from another plane and wishes to tell you of some of the studies and activities on his plane. It is the history plane; and perhaps he can tell you how knowledge comes down through the spheres. He is not a writer. I must write for him.

"He wishes to say that messages from sphere to sphere, and from plane to plane, are coming and going constantly. And, many times, century-old, or thousand-year-old communicants send down their expressions or their knowledge without coming themselves.

"You must understand that the etheric body becomes more and more etherealized as it ascends, and so comes less and less to lower planes. That is the reason that they send their intelligence, or their messages, through by spiritualized messengers on the different planes. That is the way that communications of history of thousands of years ago can come through, and how Egyptians, or Babylonians, or Hindoos, or other far-off personalities can communicate still with earth."

This is further illustrated in the chapter on Messengers, where are recorded several messages so sent.

After the above paragraphs were arranged I asked about the apparent contradictions concerning the freedom of movement between the planes.

"There are a few especially gifted and versatile ones who can move from plane to plane, although these are limited to the number of planes, as you might say—limited by their own ability of understanding or of progressing, we would say. The messengers have a relay system, as you would call it on earth, the messages being repeated from one to another without the necessity of moving beyond their power of progression."

Sis asked how an old friend in the spirit world had found her.

"The attractions on this side are more numerous and more subtle than can well be explained. But the desire to hear something from earth made him wander to the different circles which were communicating with earth. And these are not so numerous but that he could visit them all, and so he found this one. He heard your voice and was interested. He asked your name, and that is the way he found you."

There have been many people brought to us, or who have wished to talk:—friends, teachers, visitors, messengers, etc. We asked one of the friends one day:

'Do you belong to this circle?'

"No, not this circle. But I come here to get news from earth."

'A good many seem to come.'

"Yes, it is quite a 'listening post' as the army boys used to say. All are welcome. Sometimes they can only listen, but now and then one wishes to talk, and that is the way I happen to be communicating with you."

21

SPIRIT INFLUENCE

~

I remember a hymn, often sung during my childhood days, in which heaven was described as a place 'where congregations ne'er break up and Sabbaths ne'er shall end.' This was scarcely a beatific vision to an active, play-loving child, and in after years I often wondered what would take the place there of my early impression. The following may be a partial enlightenment:

"You ask what we do here. First of all, we learn the use of spirit power, after which each chooses his own work, the work for which he is best fitted. Mine is the endeavor to impress ideals upon the thought of mortals. Many spirits here are sending waves of high impulse earthward; and sometimes you see the outward manifestation of impulse in the wisdom of employer; the loyalty of employed; in the 'intellectuals' who are writing of this life; scientists experimenting along new lines; preachers, even, who are phrasing their sermons with new meaning.

"These and a thousand other beginnings are suggested from here; for the influence of this life does not move earthward in one channel only. Science, religion, art, and literature, all are impressed. A new day is coming when heaven shall draw near to earth, and the soul of man shall be baptized with spiritual gifts; and finally, finally, war and hatred shall cease on earth, and peace and kindness shall be the law of life."

'The world is surely very far from such a millennial state at present.'

"That is true; for the great masses are still immersed in selfish plans and ambitions. Yet some are pure in heart and have the vision of a purified world where brotherly love shall reign. These are the hope of the world; for the hope of the future lies truly in the philosophy that Christ brought to earth."

'Can you impress primitive people with new ideas?'

"We find ways of bringing primitive people into more of material comfort; heat in the place of cold; food for the poorly fed and poorly nourished; spiritual thought sometimes, though this is rare."

'How do you do this?'

"You know, do you not, that even animals are sensitive to impressions? Wild animals often have their physical senses so quickened that they almost reach the spiritual. Wild people live near to nature and get impressions easily at times. The Indians have thought out the 'Great Spirit,' and many of the primitive peoples have intuitions of a Being higher than themselves, and something beyond their poor lives that shall be finer and better."

'If the stimulus to progress comes from that side, why is there so wide a divergence among the different peoples of the earth?'

"Some natures have not yet evolved enough to receive. The savage has still a primitive brain. Occasionally one of their number will forge ahead and achieve fine leadership; but as a rule they are children, or less than children in spiritual life. Among the different races some started earlier in the upward climb and became ready for higher thought, while others remained entirely undeveloped."

'But the Ethiopians and the Babylonians were trading together thousands of years ago. The Babylonians made history, while the Ethiopians are practically unheard-of.'

"To advance in the comforts and luxuries of life is one thing; to advance spiritually another. The Babylonians developed brain power and used it in surrounding themselves with luxuries; yet their nature remained savage, and showed itself in cruelty and oppression. The

Ethiopians were contented to remain as they were. The hut, the out-of-door life, the spear and the hunt, were to them the best that life could give. Thus the Babylonians and the Ethiopians were one in their desire for material comfort only."

'If it is as you say, that the evil characters cannot ascend beyond the first plane until the evil has been eliminated and their characters changed into good, then there must be an overwhelming accumulation of evil on that plane?'

"There is where our occupation and responsibility come in: to prevent these evil ones from impressing their influence upon susceptible minds on earth. The evil ones here are constantly passing out of their evil thought, and becoming, if not actually constructive in good, yet neutral in influence. Yet, others with evil minds are constantly coming over, so our work is never finished."

'Do you ever become discouraged?'

"No; for we see the evil constantly changing into good, and know that the final victory will be with the good."

'How do you know that?'

"I can only say that all knowledge above us teaches that, and we have the inner conviction that comes from the Father of us all, and this can never be shaken."

In a conversation with Prof. James one evening through the pencil, he spoke of the efforts there to influence earth life. Among other things he said:

"I came over, not believing that evil and crime could exist here. But I have watched the teaching of those who are trying to help the criminals into a better life, and their work brings me into sight and knowledge of the pitiful lives and mental or spiritual suffering of those who have used their earthly existence for selfishness only, and have broken both the laws of God and man in seeking the gratification of their desires."

'Then spirit can suffer?'

"Yes; spirit is a 'sensitive' which can enjoy to the utmost, or suffer to the last degree. Which condition of spirit life shall be his, rests with the individual. How to get this truth to the selfish and to the wickedly inclined, is our problem; for their souls have become indifferent to finer impressions by the very degradation of their lives. These are the ones, however, who are influenced by the lower orders of spirit manifestations:—materialization, raps, strange sounds, and other material phenomena; and many times through these are brought into consideration of a future life. So, you see there is an influence for good in even these manifestations."

Dee told us a little of the extent of spirit influence one evening:

"I am not in the class of unbelievers as I used to be. It is all so plain here, and we have such strong impressions from the powers above that it is easy to believe where we cannot positively see or know. We are led by impressions largely, and the people on earth have far more teaching by impressions than they realize. Scientists, physicians, clergymen, inventors, are often led into far-reaching truth and skill by impressions from here. Heaven is a part of earth, and earth is a part of heaven."

In the evening of a day which we had spent in one of Nature's quiet places, this came:

"We have been with you in the silence of the hills today, and we believe you felt the presence of unseen forces. We wish we could interpret these for you. Life was there in all its varied and beautiful material dress; but the spirit that pervaded all, you could not see, and could only vaguely feel. Nature expresses the great Creative Force in manifold ways; and however people may go to this Great Teacher, it is better than to be indifferent to her manifestations. Nature is one of God's ways of speaking to the world. Many fail to define their impressions except in terms of activity. Yet there is an impression going to the inner spirit nevertheless."

22

MESSENGERS

~

THERE is a phase of spirit life, an occupation for some spirits, to which I do not remember having seen any reference in the many records of communications and descriptions I have read. This is the messenger service. Many times when we inquired for someone there we have received a reply saying, "Wait, we will send a messenger for him." Invariably there follows an interval, from a few seconds to a minute, while the pencil is motionless. Then the communication continues. Two or three times we were told that the messenger could not find the one for whom we were seeking. The interval of waiting is usually very short, and we have been told that the distances between circles and planes is sometimes very great. So it is apparent that this messenger service, which takes the place there that is filled by the telegraph and telephone here, is far more efficient than anything we have conceived, and accomplishes the work with incredible celerity. A part of the method is indicated in the first quotation given below:—the power of thought transference. But that the spirit messengers themselves go great distances is specifically stated later.

Our first information regarding them was the following:

'How do you find people there?'

"I can hardly tell you in words that you will understand, but we have messengers who can find them through ways well known here, but impossible on earth."

'A sort of mental inquiry sent out?'

"More like wireless telegraphy, but far different from that. It is operated by mind, and mind communicates with mind with the speed of electricity."

Not long afterward another reference was made to them when we asked Dee:

'If you do not reckon time there, how do you regulate the intervals between your classes?'

"A messenger announces the time and place and the children come. I meet them every day, or about what you would call a day."

In talking with a friend Sis said:

'Did you know I used an incident of your earth experience in a paper that I read?'

"It was that that brought me to you. Some magnetic communication was established by your thought of me, and I heard through my own psychic or spiritual sense that you were talking with friends here. So I sent out messengers, and, though it has been a long search, I have found you in a circle who are well beloved by those of higher spheres. Mary is a safe teacher and friend. Dee is your dearest friend and a lovely spirit. Trust them. The others I cannot see so well; but all are fine, and I am grateful that you, my friend, are cared for so wisely."

The service is further defined in the following:

"We have a very perfect messenger service and can find many people. But in the multitudes that are here we do not always get descriptions clearly enough to send for them. And then, too, they may have passed on and away from this sphere entirely. It would take an infinite mind to comprehend the infinite number here and the infinite space they occupy. Our messenger service is restricted in a way, for we call on those who are particularly the ones belonging in this sphere, and not on those who have moved on to other spheres. Many times the ones who are asked for have progressed beyond our knowledge."

That great distances are covered is explicitly stated in the following given by a messenger:

"We are the spirits of the air who go from plane to plane as messengers, and carry the thoughts of earth to friends here, and the spirit thoughts to earth friends. We have a messenger service as complete as your own mind can picture, and through this we communicate to far-off zones and spheres. We can go to other planets, or to other universes if necessary, with greater speed than those not trained in the service."

We have been told many times that each could choose his own work on that side, and many of their occupations have been described. The interest and pleasure connected with the messenger service seem to offer strong inducements to some, as the following will show:

"We will try a few sentences from one who has come to the circle for a time."

'A visitor?'

"Yes, a visiting messenger. He belongs to the messenger service and was attracted by a question you asked. Here he is:"

"I do not belong to the highest planes, nor to the very high ones, yet there is much diversity in those I visit. The messenger service is to me exceedingly attractive, bringing one into the presence of different occupations, different modes of enjoyment, and higher studies. I do not know that I can describe them to you, as you have not yet learned to understand the first plane. But knowledge grows wiser, enjoyment deeper, and wisdom greater. It is a pleasure to come into contact with the higher spirits, and the time spent in preparing for the messenger service is also a pleasure, as all acquisition of knowledge here brings its own enjoyment. The language of the highest planes is far beyond me yet, but I am able to report successfully from many of the intermediate ones."

'Do you communicate by symbols?'

"Partly, and also by translating the language or symbols of the upper spheres into the language used here."

I inquired more particularly into the requirements of the service.

"It is possible for anyone who is willing to study for the work. It might be compared with a post-graduate course there."

Many mediums claim to be controlled by spirits from past ages, and many pages purporting to be philosophy and wisdom thus given have appeared in various publications. It is possible that much of this is fraudulently given by spirits on that side who impersonate these noted sages of by-gone centuries, or is simply the imaginings of the medium's subconscious mind. Some probably is given by poor souls who have been so positive of the truth of their convictions that they have failed to advance in spiritual understanding even though centuries have passed. This is shown by our experience as related in the chapter 'Undeveloped Spirits.' Let us hope there are few who are thus delayed.

Then, as is explained in the chapter 'Circles and Planes,' there are some who really do send down messages to those on lower planes, and some of these messages are transmitted to earth. After this messenger, mentioned in the other chapter, had explained the process of this transmission from plane to plane, he continued as follows:

"I am not far away, but I am a receiver from higher planes, and so can tell you some of the things that pass through me to other planes. With whom would you like to communicate?"

'We hesitate to call for any of the great ones.' "You have the permission. 'Ask and ye shall receive';—this time at least."

'Can you tell us who communicate through you?' "You are wishing a message from Socrates. Well, here it is."

"We are on the plane where we belong. Never doubt that you will be placed correctly. We decide our position while on earth; though we may change that position by study after we have arrived. It may be that my words may become somewhat entangled in the thoughts of the different messengers through which they pass, but I will try to give you one precept that will help: "I taught by questioning, and found the weak place in the other's armor. Then one can drive at that weak place; that is a fair method. Look at all sides of every problem; question the truth at all points; find the weak place if there is one, and make use of it in the argument. Sift and sift until nothing but the truth is left. Question and question, sift and sift, and the remainder will be the truth,—that is, if there is any remainder."

Then the messenger continued:

"Do you wish another?"

'Yes, but it is difficult to know for whom to ask.'

"Will Napoleon do?"

'Do you mean that you have a message from Napoleon?'

"Yes. Napoleon sees the world slaughter of this war, and knows how his militarism fostered the cruelties and avarice and the grasping greed of nations. He knew at Elba that his life was all wrong; but did not know how to alter the greed of power, the ambition to be personally great. These dominated his personality. He came here with hardly anything left of spirituality. He was stunned by the change and by the necessity for different ideals; and long, long time passed before he could even make a beginning. Even yet he has still to struggle with the remains of the old character. His messages are always so unlike his former greed-loving self,—I mean greed for power,—that few will believe them. Can you believe this one?"

"Tell young men who seek personal power, riches, fame, and forget the rights of the lowly and dependent,—tell all such to find an Elba of their own, some desert place, some far island in the sea; and there to ponder on the rights, not of the individual, but the rights of humanity. And tell them, as they value their immortal life, to stay there until their ideals have grown pure and unselfish."

Later this messenger appeared again.

"I am a messenger from another plane. Will you tell me what you wish?"

'Are you the one who told of Socrates?'

"Yes, and can give you another message if you like,—this time from a philosopher who belonged also to the Greek civilization."

"I belonged to the very glad ones, who were glad of life, of love, of wine and pleasure."

'You mean the Epicureans?'

"Yes. We have been misrepresented. For our philosophy only tried to make the best of conditions as we saw them: Tyrants ruling the nation, riches the only power, life too short and nothing beyond. What then? Was it not a credit to make the most of the only life we knew? We did dance and feast and bid defiance to sorrow and death. But it was to us the only philosophy worthwhile. Socrates was wiser,

155

and his disciples founded a deeper philosophy; but they were sad-visaged, and many had only their thoughts to sustain them. Do not these types exist today? Only that they have not given themselves a name nor an organization."

23

MOVEMENT AND TRAVEL

~

MANY and various messengers have told of their work for, and influence with, the people of distant spheres, and have even described journeys to these remote worlds. If there is truth behind these communications, this necessitates motion with a swiftness for which we have no comparison. These references have been a continued source of wonder to me, and it is with more than usual interest that I have arranged the quotations in this chapter.

The first one is selected from our very early communications. We were talking with a lady who had passed over about the time of the advent of the automobile, and at some reference to them, she wrote:

"I never was in an automobile. I suppose they are good, but I like my way of going better."

'You have not told us how that was, that you can go so quickly. You must have wings?'

"No, child. Wings are only for pictures. We need no wings here. We go as we please, fast or slow, walk or fly, as you might say, but without wings except in thought. I mean that we move by thought more quickly than by flying."

'Is it far from this circle to your own?'

"I might call it far if on earth. Nothing seems very far here."

Dee spoke of their rapid movements also.

"We move with such ease here that we scarcely feel the motion. We can move with the greatest rapidity."

'As fast as lightning?'

"Yes, and faster, too, if we wish. You need not try comparisons, for there is nothing like it in the material world."

Another communicator spoke of going to another sphere, and we asked him:

'Is it more of a task to go to another universe than to one of our own planets?'

"I have not yet tried other universes. Higher education is needed for such wanderings. We do not arrive at all power at once, but labor for it, as earth people labor for higher gifts."

'When you spoke of going to another sphere, did you mean another planet, or just another plane?'

"I meant another sphere belonging to this planet. For the heavenly sphere belonging to this earth is of such immensity that it would mean far away indeed to go to some of its various parts."

I think it was Dee with whom we were talking when the following was written:

'You seem to have no trouble in passing back and forth to the planets?'

"No. You need never worry about accidents. Souls are not subject to them. I can go as easily as I can come here to you, but it takes longer. Spirit does not move quite as quickly as thought, but moves in a way beyond the comparison of mortals. There is a little space of time, as you call it, while we are crossing the millions upon millions of miles of space. We can move faster than light at times, but that is a matter of study. Law is in control as certainly here as there, but we can attain greater speed by studying the laws of speed and motion and vibration."

'Have you any idea how long you were on the way to Mars?'

"We probably were several hours, though we have no exact way of measuring time. All was so beautiful, and we saw so many wonders of the outer universe that I took no note of time."

'Did we get the right idea when you said you used vibrations in traveling?'

"We travel by vibrating motion through the ether. We move in vibrating action when going to distant worlds."

"We can control our speed perfectly and can move with a swiftness incomprehensible to mortals, or we can remain almost inactive in the ether."

"We have teachers who can go with the speed of spirit motion to far away spaces, and when they return they entrance us all with descriptions of the journey and conditions that are strange even to us. Speed is through vibrations far more rapid than light, or they would be many years in making the trip. The vibrations we use, and the training we receive in using them, permit a velocity unthinkable by earth computations."

Last season we were preparing for a vacation trip and were having a last visit together through the pencil. During the talk Dee said:

"You do not know the delights of traveling yet. We go as we please and we see more than you see. We see all the things that are beautiful in nature; but we do not see the disagreeable things as plainly, for they are clouded. But all of beauty and all of usefulness we can see as well as you or better.

"Travel is a wonderful educator and lays the foundation for larger perceptions. Even here we see and feel the beneficent results of travel to other planes, the coming in contact with other conditions, and the influences that form other lives and character."

A display of Aurora Borealis induced us to ask the cause. The pencil wrote in reply:

"Scientists here believe in the radium theory of heat and light in the sun."

Sis said she had seen some reference to such a theory, and I asked if it was possible that her mind was responsible for this statement through the pencil.

"Not necessarily. She does sometimes think along the right lines, and it happens that this is the case now. The theory of radium is bigger than you think, and may involve an entire reconstruction of scientific work in regard to the sun.

"This is not Mary. I was interested and—"

'Were you an astronomer?'

"I was one, or thought I was but I see so many problems from this side that my knowledge looks too small to be named at present. We study, but with far better methods and far better conditions; therefore the little I learned on earth seems hardly worth remembering now."

Sis said Mary had told of going to far universes, and that spirits could withstand the greatest heat; so she asked why he did not go to the sun and study it at first hand.

"Have you learned that we do not grasp things here without study? Travel must be prepared for by necessary study and experience of vibration force. I have not taken that yet. Many go to the planets who do not visit the sun; for the sun is not so easily approached as you might think. There are electrical and magnetic conditions that must be studied before we could venture into that blaze of heat and light. Mary says she could go into a volcano without suffering from the heat, but that does not express even in a feeble way the heat that can be intense many millions of miles away.

"I can go to the sun some time, but that time is not now.

"That is all for now. Goodbye."

'Goodbye. Will you come again?'

"I will come sometime if you don't insist that I go to the sun!"

"Mary says: He is a teacher of astronomy and is very far advanced. He just drifted in here this time without any special object, and the first we knew you were asking about the Aurora, and I turned the pencil over to him."

'Well, Mary, he can beat you in writing.'

The writing had been very large and free, quite different from Mary's characteristic back-hand.

"Mary will have to take lessons from him.

"He was right in saying that visits to the sun are not for us of this plane. That belongs to higher study and experience."

'I thought you said spirit was superior to all conditions?'

"Mary says yes to that. But spirit even must learn the laws of the universe. I do not know what would happen if some over-venturesome spirit should attempt to reach the sun. But probably it would or could not reach that point unprepared. Spirit cannot be annihilated; that I know. But there are some conditions that are still beyond our knowledge.

"We are not as independent of law as you might suppose; and it is in being in harmony with the law that we find our greatest happiness. We have tried to express some of our laws, or rather our protections,—for that is what law is here,—to you; but have not described the laws relating to advanced knowledge and higher spirit life; partly because you would not understand, and partly because we ourselves are not as familiar with them as we will be later."

We have many light touches to the conversations. Sis was talking once with an old school friend who had passed over in early life. This friend told of her work:

"I have been going on in music fast and far, and am impatient to have you here with me. We are going to be friends. Do you know it? I never realized in the old school days how closely congenial we were; but I see it now. Can you think of any studies more wonderful?"

'You are so far ahead of me. I'll never be able to catch up.'

"Do you think that will make a difference? Not a bit! I'll have the pleasure of introducing you to new emotions and new pleasures, and then—why, we can travel together! Dee says we can!"

And Mary added:

"We'll make up a party and go planet-hunting one of these days."

24

OTHER WORLDS

~

THE immensity of heaven is beyond your comprehension. We here occupy the space around the universe in which the earth is situated. But with education and training we can go to other universes when we wish. I do not know how many there are for I have never visited one, but their number is like the sands of the desert.

"We wish you to get a definite idea of our life here and its activities. To show you one phase, let me tell you that we have teachers from other planets with us who tell us of many strange and wonderful things.

"For instance, we learn that the planet Mars is inhabited by people who are different in many ways from those of earth. We cannot communicate with them in the same way, but teachers from there learn our language and tell us of their life and their surroundings.

"We learn that they are far more spiritual than earth people. They wonder at our ignorance of heavenly things, and they can scarcely understand the indifference of earth people to spiritual ideas. They have no fear of death, which to them is as beautiful as the opening of a flower. They are beautiful in appearance and in character, and their teachers here lead us up to higher thoughts. Their learning is so great that we seem like children to them. They love beauty, are gifted in music and art, and are skilled in all sciences. Because of their spiritual natures they derive much knowledge from their spirit planes.

"Mars has some problems to meet that are different from any on earth. Their water supply is obtained from subterranean sources and from the melting of polar snows. The thin atmosphere does not provide much protection, but heat and light are obtained by special electric devices. The plant life is such as is adapted to arctic regions. But so great is the care taken, and such love of the beautiful exists, that the colors and forms are varied and wonderful.

"Because of its distance from the sun the winters of Mars are long and cold. When the snow melts, the water is carried into great reservoirs and distributed through canals.

"Now you have been thinking of these canals, but you have been thinking correctly, for they really exist, though not to the extent that some have described. What is really seen from earth are the canals, bordered by roadways and a growth of forest trees. The roadways are for their marvelous system of electric travel, for they are far in advance of earth in the use of electric power.

"There is not a great variety of food, for the Martians do not eat meat. They have fruits and vegetables, but there are very few animals and none that are killed for food.

"As stated before, the people of Mars are highly educated, and cultivated in the various arts. But art is expressed differently there. Pictures are not so much in demand, because the artistic sense is developed more along architectural lines. There are many exquisite types of buildings, with ornamentation equal to the interiors of our palaces or cathedrals. Their homes are wondrously beautiful, with the rooms finished in carved picture effects."

Mary tried several times to describe this more definitely, but seemed unable to find words to express what she wished to say. Finally she wrote:

"I will ask a manufacturer from Mars to come." Then came a long pause. Finally the pencil began to write again, but in a different handwriting from Mary's peculiar backhand.

"I am a manufacturer from Mars trying to tell you through Mary about some of the things we do out there in space. We have every kind of manufactured article that can minister to the comfort of the people. We travel on earth, on water, through the air and under the earth when necessary; all devices for travel being electric, and moving with a speed and safety unknown to you.

"Mary was telling you of the houses and the intricate carvings on the walls. These are sometimes portraits, sometimes a complete story, sometimes a picture of the landscape outside. All done with great delicacy and expressing much beauty, as our artists feel the influence of beauty on the mind.

"Our climate is different from yours. We do not have the violence of nature such as you know, for everything there, material or spiritual, expresses order and symmetry. We have electricity, but it is created for our use by scientists, and does not run wild as with you in thunderstorms.

"I cannot express myself as I wish, but I can say that our manufactures include all forms of clothing for protection and adornment, made from fibers of various plants. We have no leather from animals, but use a composition designed by scientists. For choicer articles of ornamentation we make use of the precious metals as you do. I wish you could see all the beautiful things that fill our homes. I am at a loss for words to tell you of them.

"We have much literature and fine libraries. In place of newspapers the news is distributed by electricity and posted in public places. But such news is all of peaceful character, having to do with the daily lives and industries of the people.

"In the home life people are drawn together by mutual sympathies and tastes, and divorces are unknown. And under such circumstances the children develop fine and intelligent characters.

"I suppose you think this is monotonously good. If so, it is because of my lack of power to describe. Pleasures are of so many kinds and industries so varied and the love of learning so universal, that monotony is unknown."

Mary then took up the pencil and continued the message.

"Other planets are also inhabited by people formed as we are, although quite different in appearance. On Venus they do not live to what we call old age. I do not mean that they never grow old, but that they mature in a shorter time. As their years are shorter than ours, they live as many as we do, but not so long a time.

"Far from being behind us in civilization, they are much superior. They have all the best things we have and many more. They have finer organized brains, and the manner of life there creates greater development.

"The people are better looking than those of earth, and are more intelligent and more inventive.

"The heat on Venus is much greater than on earth, and life would be difficult if not for cooling devices. Cities there are built with many covered highways, and air forced through them by electric power. This power is created by new methods, which I am not allowed to explain.

"Life is far older and more advanced than on earth, but in some things they are yet quite deficient. In astronomy they are little interested. They are too near the sun for good observation. Venus has more moons than have been discovered from the earth, because the light from the sun interferes. There are many little asteroids revolving about the planet, too small to be seen from earth, but they create light at night and furnish one reason for the indifference to astronomy.

"The inhabitants of all worlds are of the same general form, but different as conditions differ. On Mars and Venus they are similar to earth people, except the Martians are larger and those of Venus smaller.

"Venus revolves around the sun as the earth does, giving the same changes of season. The surrounding atmosphere is very dense, furnishing some protection from too great heat. Many inventions exist to temper the heat, but the people are inured to the high temperatures by long habit and are rarely overcome by it.

"Venus is densely inhabited, and the occupants vary as on earth. On Mars disease is almost unknown, their passing into the spiritual life is painless and without fear. Venus also has less disease than have earth people; for there is less of the material and more of the spiritual, and it is the spirit that makes for health."

25

REINCARNATION

~

THE question of progress after the close of the material life, and, especially, continued progress throughout eternity, is a stumbling block for many in their search for truth. The old idea of complete knowledge and perfection of character for the select few who would be privileged to walk the golden streets, still clings with many, together with the idea that those who miss this happiness must spend eternity in some other place. Some believe that we are allowed another chance in a second existence on earth.

If one admits the possibility of continued progress, it is difficult to comprehend an eternity of it without reaching perfection. So, it seems, we have then three chances: an immediate perfection, a perfection reached through reincarnation, or else perfection through continued progress; a similar result in either hypothesis. But perfection is the Buddhistic idea of Nirvana, a conception very unsatisfying to many.

In these communications we are taught so earnestly that personality persists throughout eternity, that there seems to follow of necessity a different conception of perfection—not a perfection of one, but a perfection of many parts that make a whole.

This is illustrated very effectively in a presentation of the case that I read not long ago. This illustration compared the perfected whole with a complete orchestra, in which the differentiation and increased ability of each performer reached its highest attainment when each contributed most harmoniously toward the perfection of the ensemble. Thus the expression in the chapter on Progress, "always acquiring and always giving out," would mean when applied to the orchestra, "always improving the performance of each instrument, but always in a manner that most suitably adds to the general result." The more complete the individuality of each in relation to the whole, the more perfect is the whole.

If one accepts the ideas of continued progress and persistence of individuality, there is then no need for the theory of reincarnation— which, after all, is only a theory—and the quotations given below carry much force.

In a number of books which offer records of spirit communication, the theory of reincarnation is fully set forth. We were reading one of these in which the opinions of the one speaking were quite positively expressed.

It did not satisfy us, and we turned to Mary for explanation. She asked who was sending the messages.

We gave her the name and she replied: "I will send a messenger to find him and have him come to this circle if possible."

After a little while she continued: "He is here and wishes to speak. He wishes to state his own ideas on certain subjects and we have promised to let him have his say."

Then the following was written:

"I have indited several books from here, most of which are true, as I see the truth. Your instructor believes differently, so I will tell you my position. I believe in reincarnation, and I believe in evil as a living entity. … The evil go down inevitably, and as they progress in wickedness the possibility of becoming angelic decreases as a matter of course. There is no hope for them but to become reincarnated and start over again."

The writing was interrupted at this point, but another evening it was resumed.

"I am a believer in reincarnation, and in the philosophy of the Eastern Adepts. They are from birth more occult than the western world and nearer the unseen truths of life, both here and there. They believe that when a soul departs from the body it either ascends or descends according to its life on the earth plane. When it ascends it goes upward into that state of highest incomprehensible bliss called Nirvana; or it descends until the whole being becomes so evil that nothing but rebirth can start it upward again. It may reappear in the form of an animal and have all the upward way to travel over again. But it has the chance at least, of becoming a pure spirit, and so of reaching Nirvana at last."

The writing stopped and we asked: 'Then only evil is reincarnated?'

Mary replied: "He is gone, but we think that is his belief."

Then she continued: "He is strongly hypnotized by his earthly studies and beliefs, and it may be long before he comes out of them. But he will drop these ideas some time. His belief in Nirvana is the most dreary part of it—an endless inactivity of contemplating one's own bliss! The reincarnation of the evil ones is not so bad in principle, although we here cannot see how the soul can go back to animal life again, having once been human."

Then she added so emphatically the pencil nearly tore the paper:

"Our teachers from the higher planes say nothing of the kind ever happens!"

Our various readings brought up the subject several times and Mary started further:

"Many spirits here keep their belief in reincarnation for a time, and send back messages to the world stating this belief. But there is no such thing as physical reincarnation. Once a spirit, always a spirit. The progress goes on from here instead of beginning all over again in some earthly career. Some get confused in trying to tell of the intelligence. That may return to earth to help others, just as our knowledge of this life is returning to help you. Also, a few great leaders are allowed to impress their greatness upon such minds there as can receive. But try to understand rebirth as a progression only, and from that further height sending greater truths to earth. Philosophers here often carry their theories too far, just as some do on earth. That is one of the things people must learn before trusting spirit messages too completely."

She re-expressed this again:

"Many here express reincarnation as a bodily rebirth, whereas it is only a mental or a spiritual influence that returns and often surrounds a loved one there; or often enlarges the genius, or makes the wisdom higher and finer. Influence from here is constantly going earthward, but it is wrongly stated by those who believe in physical rebirth. There is no such thing, the higher teachers tell us. And surely, progress on this side is far easier than the blundering of earthly lives no matter how often repeated."

'We have not believed in it, but there seem to be some otherwise fine teachers there who teach reincarnation?'

"Do not let that worry you. Knowledge is not centered in anyone teacher. Only, I would, of course, except the divine teachings of Christ, or the higher wisdom coming from the Most High."

Again the subject was mentioned when we asked: 'Is space infinite?'

"The space called heaven has no confines, neither has creation any end. The creative power is infinite. Mind does not stop and stagnate nor lose its power of progression. Many finite minds are puzzled over the thought of eternal progression, and have fallen back on the resort to reincarnation; that is, a time of silence, and a beginning over again of a mortal life. But this is not so. We progress from plane to plane and sphere to sphere. But the mind must be in touch with infinity to realize what eternal progression and eternal occupation mean."

It is quite common for the writing to begin like the following; but this about reincarnation came as an entire surprise as we had not even been thinking of the subject for some time.

"Mary and Dee are here. What do you wish?"

'Have you anything you wish to say to us first?'

"We are not very talkative tonight. We have just been in a circle where talking seemed out of date, where we felt the silence almost oppressive. We have been in a circle where they seem possessed with the reincarnation idea, and each was trying to look backward to his other former incarnations. We had no former incarnations to study, so silence was our only act."

'Did you learn anything that you can tell us, especially how they came to believe it?'

"Mary thinks it logical enough: they cannot comprehend an unending life unless it culminates in Nirvana, and so they grasp the idea of returning circles or cycles of life on earth, a new experience each time. And this may go on indefinitely, especially in the case of wicked ones who expiate their sins by becoming animals and evolving upward through the slow-moving centuries."

'Do they not progress enough to hear your teachers?'

"No, that is the trouble. They become absorbed in the one idea and may keep it for uncounted years."

'If we have had no former spirit life, how did we begin? Is it simply by a splitting off from parent life analogous to the physical beginning?'

"I know of nothing more than that. The individual life begins with the birth of the individual, and the human being has the capacity for spirit life and the development into immortal existence. I have never studied all the philosophy or psychology of the subject. To tell the truth, it has never interested me. I love this life, I feel the upward longing, I am sure that I will progress from here and not return to the old dismal earth; so that my longings have never led me into the study of the possibilities of prenatal existence. It does not seem to me worthwhile. The reincarnationists have no proof except in their own imaginations."

26

SPIRITUALISM AND
THE BIBLE

~

MONG those who disapprove of any attempt to fathom
the mysteries of the unseen life, the ministers of the gospel
are perhaps the most earnest in counseling their followers
to avoid the entire subject. They hear of mysterious seances, of
fraudulent mediums, of weak minds tottering over into insanity;
and the whole subject seems to them bound up in deceit, fraud, and
the vain imaginings of the subliminal mind.

Yet they lose sight of the fact that the Bible itself is a repository
of psychic experiences, and they seem to forget that good and evil
have strangely intermingled since the world began; superstition,
false doctrines and fearful cruelty—as in the days of inquisitorial
practice—having many times invaded the church itself. Through
long ages it has been the effort of spiritual teachers to discern the
truth, to separate it from the false, and to draw nearer and ever
nearer the divine and absolute knowledge. Shall we not accord
the same patience and discernment to a subject which surely is of
supreme importance?

Charles L. Tweedale, an English vicar, has been so impressed with the importance of supernormal revelation, and, through his work among all sorts and conditions of men, so impressed with the conviction that a more intense and vital belief in the reality of life after death is one of the urgent needs of the times, that he has published a book, giving, first of all, the scriptural proofs of resurrection, and adding to these, psychic experiences of his own and of many acquaintances. A careful study of the Bible, he declares, reveals a record of almost continuous supernormal experiences, and these experiences he has taken pains to classify under their proper heads, as: clairvoyance, levitation, strange sounds and supernormal lights, appearances of spirit hands and the touch of discarnate beings, automatic writing, sounds of music and other manifestations. All are very similar to the psychical experiences of today. I would like to add, a little more in detail, a few of the New Testament examples that are very indicative of the good that came to the early disciples through spiritual guidance.

One instance occurs after the stoning and martyrdom of Stephen, and the bitter persecutions of the Christians immediately following. So great was this persecution that the disciples scattered, and one of them, Philip, went down to the city of Samaria to preach. While there, "An angel of the Lord spake unto Philip, saying, 'Arise, go towards the south unto the way that goeth down from Jerusalem unto Gaza, which is desert,'"—explicit directions, which Philip obeyed. And far out on this highway he saw a chariot, and in the chariot sat a trusted official of Queen Candace, the queen of the Ethiopians. A trusted official indeed, for he had charge of all the queen's treasure. He was returning from Jerusalem, and, resting in his chariot, was reading from one of the prophets. And again Philip became clairaudient and heard the words: "Go near and join thyself to this chariot." Philip obeyed the voice, and then occurred the conversation with the Ethiopian that ended in his conversion and baptism.

Perhaps more important yet is the incident told in the tenth chapter of Acts, in which a Roman centurion became both clairaudient and clairvoyant. This centurion saw in a vision "An angel of God,"—in another place described as a "man in bright clothing,"—who said to Cornelius: "Send men to Joppa and call for one Simon whose surname is Peter. He lodgeth with one Simon, a tanner, whose house is by the seaside; he shall tell thee what thou oughtest to do." Again explicit directions.

And Cornelius called two of his house servants and a "devout soldier of them that waited upon him continually",—in other words one of his body guard,—and sent them to Joppa.

But how was this message of Cornelius, a Roman soldier, to be received by Peter, a Jew, to whom it was unlawful, being a Jew, to fraternize with, or to visit one of another nation? How indeed, except through a heavenly command that was higher and more compelling than Jewish law? For Peter was on the housetop of this seaside home of Simon, the tanner, and while there "he fell into a trance,"—these are the words,—"he fell into a trance, and saw, as it were, a great sheet, knit at the four corners, and let down to earth, wherein were all manner of four-footed things and creeping things and fowls of the air." And Peter heard, clairaudiently, the words: "Rise, Peter, kill and eat." But Peter objected, saying: "I have never eaten anything common or unclean." Then the voice said: "What God hath cleansed, that call not thou common." Then Peter wondered what the vision could mean; and as he wondered, the messengers from the Roman, Cornelius, arrived, and as they waited for Peter below, once more Peter heard the voice: "Behold, three men seek thee. Go with them, for I have sent them."

Thus through spirit guidance, through vision and voice, began Peter's ministry to the Gentiles. And the power of that vision is present today, for we are Gentiles.

Saul, afterwards called Paul, a spectator at the stoning of Stephen, and he himself "breathing out threatening and slaughter" against the Christians,—went to the high priest for letters to the synagogues of Damascus, so that if he found any of the hated sect on the way, he might bring them bound to Jerusalem,—then started on his way to Damascus. And on the way, "suddenly a great light shone around him and a voice said: 'Saul, Saul, why persecutest thou me? ... I am Jesus whom thou persecutes.'" And instantly the whole inner nature of the man changed, and blinded by the vision, he was led to Damascus.

In Damascus was a devout man who by both vision and voice, was commanded to heal Paul of his blindness.

No wonder that this disciple hesitated, because of "the evil Paul had done to the Christians in Jerusalem", and a second time the command came. Then he obeyed, and Paul received his sight. And this former ruthless, cruel enemy of Christianity became, to use his own words, "obedient to the heavenly vision"; and from that time on became the apostle, philosopher, orator, skillful expounder and defender of the Christian religion.

In his ministry, led by voice and vision, he was "forbidden to preach the word in Asia", not allowed to "go into Bithynia", yet called "over to Macedonia to help"; in Corinth told by heavenly voice: "Be not afraid, but speak and hold not thy peace"; and in that wonderful shipwreck off Malta, heard the cheering words of the angel who appeared to him, saying: "Fear not, Paul, thou must be brought before Caesar, and God hath given thee all them that sail with thee."

Later, to the people of Corinth, Paul said: "I will come to visions and revelations of the Lord", and tells of "a man in Christ (whether in the body or out of the body, I cannot tell; God knoweth), caught up unto Paradise, and heard unspeakable words which it is not lawful for a man to tell."

And to the Hebrews, he speaks of their being "compassed about by so great a cloud of witnesses"; and again later, he exclaims: "Are they not all ministering spirits, sent forth to minister to those who shall be heirs of salvation?"

Was it not through this inspiration of vision and voice that the early Christians were so strengthened that they could endure the terrible privations and persecutions of that time? Is it not possible that vision and voice may in these later days, strengthen those who are working for that new day when justice and kindness shall prevail, and all nations at last be brought together in the bond of brotherhood? Is it not possible, as one has suggested, that the "second coming of Christ may mean, not that Christ shall descend into the material, but we ascend into the spiritual"?

We were speaking of the Bible one evening and Mary said:

"The essential parts of the Bible are the ethical teachings and the sacred example of the Christ. The earth needed Christ, and he came. The earth still needs him, and his influence is still here. But many are deaf and blind to this influence, and because this is so, war still desolates the earth and selfishness and crime sometimes blot out the law of unselfishness and love that he gave his life to teach."

We asked if Christ was near to those on that plane.

"Christ is exalted to the heavens above, but he is as the elder brother and the guide of us all on this plane. As you advance in knowledge of this life, we can tell you more of its mystery and loveliness."

'How can we advance?'

"Conquer doubt; build up hope; believe in the infinite love."

'The cruelties of this world and the sufferings of the innocent, make it hard sometimes to believe that the world is ruled by infinite love.'

"Believe in God's mercy through it all. The suffering of the innocent is more than made up to them here.

"The pure in heart have a vision of a purified world where kindness and justice shall reign. They are the hope of the world, and through them we must reach those whose thoughts are all for self and for selfish interests.

"The hope for the future lies in the philosophy that Christ brought to earth and which here is our rule of life. Christ was the apostle of love and patience, and he desired to deliver the world from evil through the power of love. But evil held sway by reason of its long continuance and growth, and was too strong, as it has many times since been too strong, to be overcome by spiritual power. But the time is coming when the Christ love will prevail, and wisdom and love together shall rule the world."

One Christmas we asked for a Christmas thought, and the pencil wrote:

"We know that you are remembering the birth of Christ on this day, and we believe that both birth and death should be remembered sacredly and reverently, but the life is more to humanity than either. The world should concentrate its thought more on his life with its wonderful wisdom and love."

27

MISCELLANEOUS

~

S OME information has been received on a number of subjects that are difficult to classify under other headings. The following probably include the most important statements:

'Are angels different from other spirits?' "The spirits of mortals are different from the angelic host. The angels are more perfected, and belong to a higher organism than we at present have. You may call it a higher form, a more progressive state. Many higher forms already exist, and many more are progressing.

Consider the eternal progression that is going on in every planet, and how essential the higher forms of life are there, to forward that progression. The angels were once mortal, some on earth, some on other planets. But the many years of their spiritual life in the celestial world have given them a wisdom and knowledge and perfection of character, that we of the lower planes have not yet achieved. Therefore we do not speak of ourselves as angels; only as spirits moving along the upward way.

"Angels are not connected with earth-bound spirits as we are. They are moving to other and higher studies and activities. Mary has preferred to stay here, and many are like her. We find abundant opportunities for service here. We are attracted to the planet we came from, and prefer to stay near it for a time."

We inquired concerning two who went over as infants, and were told:

"They are not pure spirits yet, for then they would belong to the angelic host. They came as infants, but they possessed the immortal spirit, and they differ only in the fact that they have never known sin nor earthly life,—material life I should say."

'What do you have that they do not?'

"We have the knowledge of good and evil, and the power of choice, and the education through this to help others who are still in a world of good and evil. But there are many other ways in which they can serve."

These infant spirits are infants no longer, for they have been there many years. They wrote one evening:

"We think it interesting to watch these messages to and fro. Can you give us a thought from earth now?"

I don't know that this should have surprised us, but it did. We all at once realized that they knew nothing of earth or material things by experience any more than we knew spirit life by experience. Sis asked if they could not see material things.

"They are untrained in that respect. What they would like to know is how you manage to live with all those earthly impediments they hear about."

I asked if they had ever been brought in contact with evil on that side.

"Not much. They could not become teachers, for they have no earthly experience. Their work is along other lines. They are trying hard to understand earth life, but many of its phases seem unbelievable to them. The crime and cruelty they only know by descriptions, but they look at it as an almost unbelievable fiction. They do not fully realize it any more than you fully realize this life.

They have been taught and believe it as you believe some far away facts of ancient history. Perhaps that is not a good comparison either; for you have at least some other earthly happenings to compare it with. But they have not; so it is hard for them to understand."

Many months later we were talking with them again and the following was written:

"We are learning the earth language and often listen to the conversations between you and the circle. It seems very wonderful to us, very wonderful that people on earth are willing to live in the midst of such sin, misery, sickness, ignorance, and poverty, and all the other ills we hear you describe."

'Do you not see the ignorant and criminal ones who come over there?'

"We are not really in touch with them, for we do not try to influence the earthborn mortals when they first come over. Our work with them is afterward in trying to help them to the various occupations here."

'You seem to come together; are you together all the time?'

"Mary says: They came over so young that they received most of their education together and they grew into a companionship that has become a habit as well as a joy. They are alike in temperament, so that naturally they grew into intimate companionship."

I asked if such infants reached maturity earlier there than here.

"Yes, because they learn more rapidly. One of them came over several years before the other, as you know. He was far more mature than if he had remained on earth for that time. He met his little brother and was his helper for a long time, and his father taught him to love the family tie wherever congeniality existed. Then they took up studies together because both were interested in the same things."

'Having no sin nor selfishness to overcome, I should have thought they would be on a higher plane by this time?'

"They could go at any time, and they are connected with circles who are studying higher things; but their father preferred to remain near the earth plane, and they have loved him and stayed with him."

'How does the earth appear to them?'

"Mary says: They look upon it as a mystery and—"

"Will you listen to them?"

"We are not able to comprehend many things. We hear of the mechanical devices there and wonder much about them. We move in a flash of time. You are studying ways of getting about upon the surface of the earth, in the air, on the water, or maybe under the water. We have heard of your submarines and airplanes, automobiles and railroad trains. It all seems so slow, so difficult, so unnecessary! How do you ever find time to move from one place to another! Then you have to spend so much time in sleep; and Mary tells us that you have to spend time and strength and money in providing things to eat and drink. How can you be patient with it all?"

'Have you studied the earth enough to be able to sense or understand material things as compared with your spiritual objects?'

The reply seems to us to show that they do not fully understand, for they still refer to actions rather than to things.

"We try to understand. We try to move as slowly as your fastest travel and we grow impatient. We can have some sensation of taste, but we cannot understand how people would ever be willing to spend much time at it. We have tried our best to sleep, but we could not succeed, and can only guess how that is accomplished. You see we are handicapped when we try to help earthborn persons when they first arrive here."

"Ghosts are the uneasy spirits who have left some earth duty undone, or some wrong unrighted, and they try to go back again. The spirit of one who has committed a crime, or who has wronged someone on earth, is never at rest until the wrong is made right. Let this be a lesson to evil doers. There are uneasy souls here who never have peace because they cannot undo the wrong. Criminals learn the lesson too late, and if reincarnation were true they would gladly go into another earth life to profit by the lesson they have learned here. We wish we could make this plain to all evil doers."

'You say they never have peace. Do you mean that literally?'

"We mean it in connection with mortal life. Of course the one who has suffered comes here sooner or later, and then the opportunity arrives for righting the wrong.

"We have many here who are making a study of these wandering spirits, and it is found that they sometimes seem to be seeking lost treasure which to them is of transcendent importance."

'With the infinite number who have gone over, space must be well occupied?'

"Not all space, for there is no limit to space."

'In the far, far distance, do the stars thin out or come to an end?'

"I am told there is no end. All earthly vision ends, but not the universe."

'Do you comprehend infinity better than we do here?'

"Many, many things are beyond our comprehension yet; but we grow toward the larger understanding by degrees. Would you have all knowledge at once? If all things opened out to you at once, what would you do throughout all eternity except to long for something new? No! Knowledge is always progressive, and the farther we go, the broader the outlook; the more we learn, the more infinite seems the knowledge beyond."

The following quotations from our records indicate somewhat the interest that communication arouses on that side. Incidentally, the skeptic will have some difficulty, I think, in explaining how or why they originated in the subconscious mind of the psychic, which, of course, is where such critics would be inclined to place them.

Without other introduction the pencil began to write:

"A visitor from another plane wishes to talk. He is interested in our work and wishes you to tell him some of the reasons why communication between the two worlds should continue."

'Is it new to him?'

"Yes, he has never been brought into contact with it on his plane. He left no very strong ties on the earth plane, so he asks in all seriousness why there should be such communication."

'Have you not told him your reasons?'

"Yes, but he wishes yours also."

'We think the principal reason is to furnish proofs of the reality of a future existence.'

"That is of great importance, he admits."

'Another reason is to impress mortals that they are preparing their future life now and should be made aware of it.'

"Yes; he admits that also."

'Did he have no fear of death?'

"No, he had no fear; but he sees that it might be a sad thing if one anticipated either annihilation or the everlasting punishment that was a part of the old creed."

'We feel that there is a growing loss of faith in the truth of the Bible and therefore a loss of faith in a future life. Communication might supply material for renewing that faith.'

"He never doubted the Bible and so never knew that such proof was necessary."

'We have so many foreigners who seem to have little faith in a future life, such as anarchists and others who denounce the Bible entirely, or others who have beliefs formed on the creeds prevalent in their own countries. Anything that would convince them would be of value.'

"These are all arguments that he sees now, but he did not realize the need while there. He lived a moral life with sufficient belief in this life to be comfortably hopeful and fearless of the future; so that the black wall of an unknown eternity had never appeared to him. As he believed in the Bible and in the church, and was a worker in his church associations, he believed these sufficient for anyone. Therefore he had no need for any knowledge beyond the teachings of the church.

"He wishes to know what the clergymen think of the subject?"

'Unfortunately many of them are opposed to such teaching.'

"He has been here a long time and has not watched the overturning of old creeds. Neither did he realize the vast multitudes coming into your country from heathen lands or from lands where religion was largely a matter of form, ritual, and creed."

'Does he see the force of these arguments?'

"Yes, he says he can see. And as you state your view point he begins to feel that the work is necessary and must go on. It is sometimes necessary to convince spirits on this side, of the value of the work of communication. You no doubt remember that a clergyman here some time ago asked some of these same questions. This clergyman has now become very earnest in his desire to help and he is often in this circle studying methods. We realize the value of all helpers in the work of spiritual teaching. There are all too few of these; too many are looking for other things:—writing through mediums, attempting materializations, and giving messages that neither inspire nor teach."

Several months later the following was received on the same subject:

"Will you listen to one who wishes to talk to you? He is not an acquaintance, but wishes to know the sensation of talking to someone on earth again, for he has never communicated since he has been here, and that has been long. He wishes to know if you believe fear of death can be conquered by means of communication?"

'We feel and believe that many would lose such fear if communication is absolutely proven. Would you not think so?'

"He hears through Mary and answers through her. He does not hear earth sounds yet for he has had no experience. He is interested now for the first time. I have repeated to him what you have said. He says that such conversations must take away the fear of death, because in themselves they are a proof that there is no death.

"He asks now what you consider the moral value of such work?"

'We fear that much, if not most, that comes across does harm; but possibly the little that is true does enough good to counter-balance.'

"Mary does not endorse that, even knowing, as she does, the foolish and false things that are supposed to be messages. You hear more of these than of the quiet and spiritual help that is being asked for and received at all times."

'What do you think is the moral value, Mary?'

"First of all, to energize the spirit life on earth; second, to teach that life there is preparing the life here. In short, to vitalize all earth life with spiritual thought and perception."

'Does this visitor hear this?'

"He listens, and thinks we may be right; but he is slow to receive new thought."

'Why has he not known of the work of communication?'

"Heaven is immeasurable in space and infinite in its occupations and variety of interests. Not all care to commune with earth; many have never tried, even in the centuries they may have been here.

"He will ask one more question. Can sinners be saved and sin overcome by the union of heavenly and earthly influence?"

'We think so; but, Mary, will you not answer that question also?'

"Yes, and always yes, Mary says. But not under the present conditions of mediumship in general. There is too much self in both receiver and sender, there is too much desire for earthly benefits. All this must disappear, and the true longing for the heavenly life must appear in both sender and receiver. Then a power could be established which would turn souls away from selfishness and draw the world into the brotherly love we hear so much about."

Still another personality appeared one evening with questions for us to answer. He proved to be an earnest student after information, but his first questions aroused our suspicions as to the sincerity of his inquiries. The whole interview was an entire surprise; and, like the previous quotations, should cause the skeptic to think long and carefully, if he is inclined to place their origin in the subconscious mind of the psychic.

Sis took up the pencil with the intent to ask Mary some questions, but there was no wait for them. The pencil began at once:

"Will you take a message from one who wishes to communicate?"

'Is it anyone I know?'

"Will you try to listen to what he says?"

'Is this Mary?'

"Will you try to take his message?"

'Who is writing? Are you anyone whom I know?'

"Will you try to take his words?"

'I want to know who is writing first.'

"He is known here as a student of theosophy, and would like to tell you of his conclusions."

'I would like first to know just who you are.'

"Will you be patient while he explains?"

'Are you the ancient spirit that once tried to write?'

"No; I am not the one whom Mary refused to allow. I am a student of many things and am very interested in the various beliefs of the future, for even here there is room for different beliefs and creeds. I am not convinced of the ways of eastern philosophers, yet their reasoning is often eloquent and persuasive. What do you believe is the final condition, or the ultimate fate of the soul?"

'I do not believe the eastern philosophy, but rather that there is progression on that side as on this, and that the progress continues indefinitely.'

"Will that theory be received by logicians do you think? Will you tell me if many there believe in eternal progress? Will you tell me your reasons for believing it?"

'That is what we have been taught from that side and it appeals to our reason.'

"Is it better than a state of heavenly calm and happiness—Nirvana? Or better, even, than a return to earth to live out other and higher lives?"

'But we are told that the soul does not return to earth?'

"That is the opinion of many wise ones here. I am asking for the wisdom of the earth mind and desire only?"

'Many here, of course, believe in reincarnation; but it seems so much more reasonable to us that progress goes on from there, rather than to come back into the sins and sorrows of this world to try to progress. It would seem to offer much more happiness to leave all earthly troubles behind forever.'

"That is admirable, and looks like true happiness; but I wonder if it is the truth?"

'Cannot you find out if it is the truth?'

"I am interested in developing myself by study and by contact with the thoughts and beliefs of others."

'Then why do you not seek the highest teachers there?'

"I shall sometime, and will apply myself closely. But at present I am trying to get at some consensus of earth opinion."

'If I were looking for higher things, trying to learn of final conditions, I would not look backward to earth conditions.'

"You do not quite understand me, I am sure, and perhaps it is not necessary. But if one should be a teacher of the progress of life on earth, would he not begin with the lower forms?"

'Are you a teacher?'

"I am trying to prepare myself for a teacher, and have a certain delight in the evolution of belief in the past, and the probable evolution of belief in the future."

'I still wonder that you do not try to get this from teachers there?'

"Will you believe that I am not a foolish inquirer. I am truly working along the lines that I have described. The spirits here have evolved too far to be a beginning of such history, and I have wished to go back to the earth and start at the beginning. You are a long way from the beginning, but yet a link in the great chain of evidence. How I wish I could show you the infinitely subtle and varied changes from age to age, from soul to soul, each age leading a little higher in effort and belief, each age overcoming much of superstition and ignorance. Just now belief and faith on earth are being made so complex by the shadings of philosophy, psychology, and other new thought, that it is hard to move on or up in a straight line. But I tell you the study is fascinating, and so you will see it some day.

"You are looking for an abiding place for your faith. I am studying the different phases, or 'abiding places' which have served for millions of years. I am not frivolous, I am interested, and preparing to help others on this side when I can."

'Well, it has seemed to us to be far more satisfactory to go on developing ourselves, our personality, our individuality, continuously on that side, rather than to strive for a state of calm, an eternity of perfection where one, as Mary has said, would have nothing to do but to contemplate one's own bliss.'

"You have said it! To all of which I say, Amen!"

'Then why are you a student of theosophy?'

"Well, are you not interested sometimes in even heathen rites? I am."

'Yes, certainly, as a matter of history.'

"Well then you can guess the interest I have in this study."

'I still wonder what is your opinion of the final goal?'

"We are not told definitely. Do you think there would be much interest in life if every step of the future could be seen? Would not life pall and become uninteresting? We are left much of the old adventurous spirit; we are constantly stimulated with the problems that appear before us. And because the earth people cannot understand, they cavil at the difference of opinion expressed on this side. They do not know that because of the freedom of thought and study on this side our lives are full of tremendous interest. To learn! To know! To choose the best and wisest! That is life!"

'Was the 'daemon' of Socrates his spirit guide?'

"His guide took the form of a spirit, and was near to protect him; but did not suggest any course of action. That was left to Socrates's own judgment. That is where the free will comes in. "There are influences from here, but they are not strong enough to sweep human life into them. The spirit within each life is the deciding power as to which influence shall be received. Otherwise life would lose its power of choice, its free will, and its responsibility.

"There are influences constantly going out towards humanity from here. There are inspirations toward good; there are sinister suggestions toward evil; and it is the inherent choice of the individual that decides which shall rule his life."

'Just how much can you foretell?'

"Not much. We can see circumstances and the probable results, and many are able to tell the future somewhat from them. But I do not think I am gifted in that way. Some people seem to have a gift of prophecy; yet it is a psychic gift, or possibly a keen intuition, that can foresee results from certain conditions.

"We are not creatures of fate. Set that down as a truth not to be denied. What the prophetic gift is, I do not know; but we are free to live our own lives. The future is not ours. Yet we listen with eager interest to our higher teachers who bring to us glad tidings and joyful outlook for the future. But whether this future is far away or nearby, is more than we can tell."

"We do not understand the prophetic gift any more than you do. We have thought it was the gift of farseeing from the surrounding circumstances. If there is something more than this there is something more for us to discover."

'What do you know about the 'fourth dimension'?'

"The fourth dimension is as improbable here as there; mostly a problem for mathematical minds to puzzle over. Maybe I am mistaken, but I have never heard of it here, or seen any evidence."

'I suppose you do have three dimensions?'

"Will you give up your idea of our nothingness. We are good solid spirits! There now!

"The puzzles of this life are beyond those of the mortal thought. There are plenty of enigmas to solve here, you will find. Only that, when found, they are seen to be a truth so valuable that it is essential in some way to our life and happiness."

'What do physicians find to do there?'

"Plenty and plenty. Those who come over mentally unbalanced, those needing kind and wise treatment to bring them out of sin or out of selfishness, and those who are projected into this world by accident or suicide or other sudden ways, all need spiritual physicians. The remedial agencies here are mental and spiritual instead of material; but physicians, if of the right stamp, soon learn to adapt their treatment to such cases."

'What happens to the mind that has been unbalanced here?'

"We have many specialists who take charge of these. Many are the result of disease or old age, but those are easily cured. For spirit does not require any gray matter or brain cells for intelligence.

"Sometimes a snap in the brain or in the arteries, and they come to us very quickly. In such cases it is without knowledge that they have passed out of the body. That is a condition that has to be watched and cared for here, else they remain very long in the dream state and do not progress. I have watched many cases on earth but never knew what happened on this side until I came here. Physicians have work to do here. And their labor on earth, and their study of abnormal conditions there, help them here to heal the spirit that is beclouded by the physical; or, rather, the impressions made by the physical while it had power over them. Spirit is very impressionable while on earth, and some of the impressions often remain for a time after they arrive here."

Very early in our efforts with the Ouija-board a personality appeared one evening who moved the little tripod in a different manner from the others, and it spelled out:

"I am not lovable, for I am old and homely. I am not lacking in intelligence, but I would never take a prize at a beauty show."

After this whimsical introduction he continued slowly:

"All aspirations are lofty according as they are constructive or destructive."

"Fate is only another name for organized purpose."

"Life purposes may be good or evil; but eternal purpose is always good."

"All good impulses are but the expression of latent purpose."

"All constructive actions there are a help against the forces of evil."

"Continue to study life's mysteries and you will accomplish all you wish for good."

"Death gives a new and broader field, makes life more livable."

"Life is continuous."

"Keep in a judicial mood, for life asks many decisions."

"All actions in the life there help to form the life here."

"Life and love create a need for continuance of existence."

"A yearning for immortality is implanted in every individual."

These epigrams were quite a source of astonishment to us. They were given without other preface or explanation. But we were still more astonished later when one evening Ouija spelled:

"Dee."

"The death of the body is the chance for life to have its fullest expression."

"Use happiness to further happiness."

"Hope for great things, and you will not get small things."

"The best actions are those that make for happiness of persons who have less happiness."

"Good only makes for good; evil makes only for disintegration."

"The happiest spirit is that which has always caused nothing but happiness."

"Have much charity for him who is trying to rise, though he may at times slip."

"Use much care in thinking, and the actions will not so often be in vain."

At another time we asked for more such thoughts to open a new record book. Dee at first said she could not give any, but we insisted, and after quite a wait she spelled:

"Make no rays of light to pass through darkness unless they are tempered to the eyes that dwell in darkness."

"Hate so robs reason that the mind renders worthless judgments."

"Gentle thoughts often create strong ideas in the thinker's mind."

"Happiness is only soul contentment."

"Give no cause for sorrow and you will have no cause for sorrow."

"Gestures and words sometimes tell things that the mind does not voice."

"With an opportunity for knowledge, a fool only will say:—I hasten away."

The board ceased its motion for a time and as it started again we could almost hear Dee draw a long breath as she said:

"That is enough for this warm evening. Try some yourself."

Nearly two years later I was talking about these epigrams and was wondering how Dee came to give them. Sis was sitting with pencil in hand, so she asked if Dee heard what I said.

"Dee is here. I heard you talking about my wisdom of earlier days. Tell him it was not my wisdom at all. I was studying with a wise teacher, studying the philosophy of life, and some of his sentences impressed me so much, I repeated them to you."

'I see. We took them almost letter perfect, did we not?'

"Yes, I am sure you did."

28

A SPIRIT TESTIMONY

~

SCORES of people, mostly old friends and acquaintances of Sis, have at different times been brought to us and introduced in various ways. The following quotation from our records includes a very interesting message from one of these friends. The writing commenced one evening without any previous indication of the identity of the personality.

"Will you listen to someone who wishes to talk to you?"

'Is it someone whom I know?'

"Will you take a message and judge for yourself?

"He is a friend of olden time and wishes to look back upon the earth life as it was when he left it many years ago. He was not in your home town as a resident, but often came there, and knew you in your home before your mother moved to the last house she lived in."

Up to this point Sis was wholly in the dark as to the personality behind the pencil; but in a flash she saw the possibility of a test:— "not a resident," "but often came there," and "knew you in your home before your mother moved to the last house she lived in." That change of residence had occurred many years ago. With a sensation of great incredulity she waited for the information which would prove these three statements either true or untrue. The very next sentence confirmed them all:

"He says he used to play the violin with your piano accompaniment."

'Why,' she exclaimed, 'you must be Mr. S?'

Mr. S was a violinist who frequently came to the town on business, and he had acquired the habit of bringing his violin with him. He at once replied:

"Yes; it is I. I have thought of you often, and have wished to find you, but never knew how until I chanced upon this circle. Mary was talking with you, and I listened as to a stranger at first; but when your questions came across they sounded like some you used to propound to me that I couldn't answer. In curiosity I asked who was talking and learned it was you.

"California is a long way from S, but not so long as the step into the dark that I took from earth life to this."

'You were so musical when here; you must be interested in it there?'

"You know how I loved it; but when I came over I was so dazed that for a long time even music left me. I had never thought seriously of this life; I feared the change and tried to put it out of my mind. I came rather suddenly; a sudden cold, pneumonia, a brief illness, and I was here. Will you try to conceive what it was to come without a moment's real preparation or any true idea of this life. Will you try to conceive the dense and unnecessary ignorance and fear. That is the tragedy of it all. Fear is so unnecessary and the change is so beautiful, if only one could hold the true spiritual thought and life there. I do not mean preaching and praying necessarily, but just a generous loving life of trying to help one's fellow men and cultivating a belief in a larger and better life here. I did not have any warning particularly; it was all so sudden, and my mind was bewildered until unconsciousness came. Then I seemed to myself to be dreaming a beautiful dream, and in this dream selfish thought and purpose seemed to drift away and a new soul seemed to be born. That was when I really was here, without my knowing that I had passed across the Great Divide. After a time my dream seemed to change into a reality, and I was semi-conscious of friendliness and care surrounding me; and then, after a little, I awoke to full consciousness, and found that I had died, as they say there,—but as I say, found that I *lived* for the first time.

"My first sensation, perhaps, was the feeling of utter and delightful freedom and lightness of the body. This brought the sense of supreme happiness. Will you know that as much as I loved music it did not come at first; I had to go through the preparation for spiritual hearing and other spirit senses. It is all strange and all wonderful, and to me all beautiful and natural; though a few earth-born souls are rebellious and unhappy at first over the loss of their mortal senses and occupations.

"After a while I began to hear sounds; and music, soft and gentle at first, seemed to pervade the air. Then I knew that some day I could be what I always longed to be on earth,—a musician. I am in the music circle here, and love it—love it more than I did on earth, and you know how much that means."

'I suppose you do not play a violin there?'

"There are no violins proper; but the effects are enhanced here in other ways until one does not miss the particular instrument. I do not know that I can describe the instruments or their tones; but compare them to the grandest or the sweetest or the most compelling music you have ever heard, and then multiply the impression a hundred fold, and you may get a faint idea of the heavenly music.

"Will you answer me one question? What are your thoughts concerning this life?"

'Has not Mary told you of our conversations?'

"Yes, they tell me of the long talks you have had with them; but I wish I could give you a realization of life here, for that is what I so needed when on earth. It would be a great balance to any life, and particularly to one of a nervous, sensitive temperament."

'Can you tell how long you have been there?'

"No; we do not count time in the old way, but live in the present. It is always the present, for the future is so secure and safe that we have no fear. Do you realize how much fear was a part of our existence there? Loss of health, of friends, money, position, even life itself, haunted us even while we were outwardly happy and cheerful. That was my experience, at all events.

"What can I tell you of this life to add to your pleasure in looking forward to it?"

'I have been told that spirit sound can be heard at long distances; if there is so much music, how do you shut it out when you wish other sounds, or wish for silence?'

"Heaven is not all sound. There are great spaces of silence, where sound cannot disturb the other occupations. Therefore the circles of music are located in such ways as never to disturb. This is not always by distance; there are ways of preventing sound from annoying or hindering other occupations. Then, too, one can make himself immune to sound in a great measure. Mind is both the revealer and the secreter, if I may use that word. Nothing is forced upon anyone's attention."

Some difficulty was experienced in getting through another sentence and Sis asked:

'Am I doing this myself?'

"No, you are trying to help me out in a difficult explanation. Conditions are so different here, it is hard to explain satisfactorily anyhow.

"You will listen to music when you wish and you need not be disturbed by it when you are occupied in other ways."

'You were rather grave and serious as I remember you.'

"You are right in saying that I was not easily moved to laughter. I was habitually grave, and often melancholy; the future was my haunting specter; ill health, poverty, loneliness, and death haunted my vision of the future, and I had no assurance of anything better. For, while I had a vague feeling that the broken hopes,—the disappointments of earth,—might find some compensation after that life was over, I could not actually believe or see how such compensation could come. 'The light that never was on land or sea' came to me only after the sleep that men call death. Can you realize how I live in the blessed present, knowing that neither illness nor loss can cloud my future?"

29

A MESSAGE

⁓

A NUMBER of times we have presented some of the
results of our writing before a group of friends who were
interested in what we were doing. At these meetings
one or both of us gave a talk or lecture which was followed by
remarks and discussion by the audience. Much of the matter in
these earlier talks is included in previous chapters. In the following
chapter I am recording one that Sis gave, and I am presenting it
in Sis' own words:—

I wish to bring to your notice three communicators who have
appeared to us, and I would like to bring them to you in just the way
that they came to us, because the manner of their coming seems to
me, at least, to be more or less evidential. The appearance of one
of these shows a unique personality, and I am going to describe it
before giving the only message I have received from him, which,
suddenly discontinued over a year ago, has been just lately as suddenly
resumed and completed.

It was early in our work, while we were still experimenting
with Ouija, that a friend sat opposite me at the board, while F. R.,
nearby, wrote down the letters as they appeared. Ouija had been
very unreasonable that evening, giving us only a jumble of words

and sentences, so that when it spelled the same group of letters without pause three times, F. R. thought it only another piece of foolishness.

"HALEVANSHALEVANSHALEVANS."

Still, we went on. But when it spelled "AS WE DISH," then a lone "C," followed by "HE MIST," F. R. exclaimed:

"This is just nonsense. We can't get anything tonight."

My friend, however, looked at the paper then for the first time, and had a sudden inspiration.

"Why," she said, "that spells 'A Swedish Chemist'!"

And above, concealed in the three times repeated letters, was evidently his name, 'Halevans.' We did not hear the Swedish chemist laugh, as he undoubtedly did, but afterward when we spoke of his puzzling advent, he wrote through my pencil:

"Yes, I nearly missed the trick that time!"

He said little that first evening, except to declare that what was known of chemistry on earth was but child's play compared to the science as revealed in the life beyond. But some time later he came again saying that he wished to give a message. And the message was begun; but it proved a very difficult one for me to take as it was quite out of my line of thought. Also, the Swedish chemist proved an exacting and, as I thought, impatient personality, often disappearing after a sentence or two, because not satisfied with my transcription.

Finally, I too, grew impatient, and wished no more of this exacting Swede! After a number of evenings, and when there had been several pages of the message written, Halevans disappeared, and for more than a year his writing remained unfinished. Finally one evening I said:

"I believe I will ask to have another communicator from that sphere finish the message of Halevans."

This brought the chemist to the fore again; and an evening or two later, my pencil wrote:

"I am here. I will tell you what I wish. It is to have you finish my message in words of my own choosing.

"Halevans."

After one or two ineffectual attempts he rapidly finished it. When it was done he wished me to read the entire message for his correction. This I did, and he altered a few words and phrases and omitted some sentences. So now I am able to read the message to you with the corrections of its author.

The second personality added a few sentences to Halevans' message in an explanatory way, and, as I wish to read the message with his additions, I will introduce him before commencing.

In the first place I am going to ask you how clear a memory you would have of people whom you met casually, and only once, twenty-five or thirty years ago.

They come and go, do they not?—a moving throng, scarcely leaving an impression on your brain. That, at least, is my experience, and that is why the coming of this second personality seems also to me to belong among the evidential occurrences.

One evening several pages of exceedingly interesting matter was written, ending rather abruptly with:

"That is all for now. Who am I? Do you know?"

"No, I haven't the slightest idea. Are you anyone whom I have known?"

"Try to think of the name of a teacher of natural history in a college of your home state."

"Well, Prof. Agassiz is the only name I think of now?"

"Professor Agassiz was a noted teacher, and I should be proud to own the name, but I am not he."

"You say you taught in a college?"

"Yes, and not at Harvard."

"Do you mean Williams College?"

"Yes; that is the one."

"I knew one A S of Williams College, but I think he was a student rather than a teacher."

"I am not he, but I knew him well."

"I am sure I do not know who you are."

"I spent some days once in your hometown and heard you at the organ in church."

"Oh, I wonder if you are the friend who visited Mr. N once?"

"Yes, now you have it."

"I remember taking a ride one afternoon when you were in the party, the only time that I met you. If you are the one I have in mind you went to Florida shortly afterward, but did not live long?"

"Yes, I went there, and only lived a short time afterward."

"You have been on that side a long time, then?"

"Yes; a long time, and am only a beginner in learning yet."

Now I will introduce number three, as the three all have a part in the message I am about to read.

Some of you may have seen the articles in the Cosmopolitan magazine, written by Basil King, in which he gives some interesting philosophy received from an intelligence whom he called Henry Talbot, stating that this name was used to hide the real identity of the transmitter. I read all the articles, and afterwards wondered many times who the wise Henry Talbot might be.

One evening it occurred to me to ask of the one who seems to be our special instructor, if she could tell me the real name of Henry Talbot. My pencil wrote slowly:

"W-i-l-l-i-a-"

And then, as I saw it was going to write William, I drew my hand away, because I had somehow thought of Talbot as among the great names of the past, and no such ordinary name as William appeared to me to be right. There was a pause of a few seconds and then my hand was moved down the page a little and wrote:

"He was a teacher of psychology."

My brain did not connect the two until F. R. looked at the writing and said:

"William, teacher of psychology? William James, of course."

I hardly believed that I had the name correctly, and turned to the pencil for information, asking our instructor, Mary Bosworth, if the name had been given to us correctly. The pencil wrote:

"I will call him if you wish."

After a short pause it again wrote:

"This is Henry Talbot, and I am William James. What can I tell you to convince you of my identity? You were just now thinking of my book, *The Will to Believe*. That book seems rubbish to me now, for here all doubt is forever set at rest and clear understanding prevails."

The mention of his name had brought the book to my mind.

"In your communications to Basil King you talked about the souls of inanimate things. Was that received correctly?"

"I am not sure," he wrote, "for I did not read the copy afterwards. I suppose I have something of the poet's feeling for the lower orders of creation, but I ought to differentiate that feeling from the absolute truth perhaps, because the life in these inanimate things does not reach up to intelligent beings and to the immortality of the soul. You will realize though, a certain consciousness—shall we call it intelligence?—in vegetable forms, in their pushing toward the light, and in their search for water; and in the vine that reaches out for support that may be far away. What this intelligence is I do not know, but something there is in every living thing that betrays some sign of consciousness. It was that that I was trying to express."

After commenting on this I said:

"I remember that you used the word rhythm many times in speaking of that life. Will you tell me just what you meant by it?"

"It is a meaning that I cannot convey readily to human perception. It belongs to the vibrations that we become conscious of here, but a consciousness gained only on this side."

"I asked Mary once," I said, "what rhythm meant as applied to that life, and the answer of the always practical and sensible Mary was: 'Rhythm is a term used by transcendentalists; maybe they know what they mean, but we don't.' "

"Mary has a lot of good, hard sense. Trust her and go ahead."

While all this was interesting, there was nothing that established the identity of Henry Talbot. But some months later we learned that a Boston newspaper had published the statement that Henry Talbot was Prof. William James, and, from other information that we have received, there remains no doubt of the truth that they are one and the same personality.

And now, after this long preamble, I will read Halevans' message.

"I desire to say first, that I wish you to have the open mind, without preconceived ideas. I will explain as I go along.

"First, then, is the cosmos itself, and the particles composing the cosmos. The smallest portions of matter are what you call electrons. We here call them 'grains of force.' These ultimate particles are infinitesimal portions of universal force, and are united by some power to create an atom. From atoms molecules are formed. There are also segregated atoms. These are the beginnings of individual life. The creation of the life atom is due partly to electricity, yet the Great First Cause is behind and beyond all life, all atoms, all grains of force.

"I will begin with the cosmic forces as we find them on the earth planet. Let me explain the word cosmos, for it contains everything in life, big or little, and is the world and the universe as well.

"Forces, greater than the mind can conceive, are constantly building in the great unknown spaces. The grains of force that belong to chemical action are not the source of life, but are the foundation of the material world. The source of life is far more spiritual even than these invisible particles, and is the gift of the great Creator of us all. A starting point is hard to find; for life is elusive,—that is, the germ of the life principle. What I can do is to take the given quantity, the life germ, and build from that. This life germ, once established, goes on in infinite gradations, through mollusc to animal, through animal to man, through man to spirit. After spirit comes immortality and endless progression.

"To begin with the living organism in its first inception, we must go back in the scale of creation,—farther back than you are aware; because the germ of life belongs to the invisible creations that even microscopic examinations have failed to reveal. Among these infinitely small forms is one that bears within, the germ of the human life. Cast out on the sea of life, it changes, enlarges, and multiplies, until a mollusc lies within its shell. From this unthinking, unseeing form, in the evolution of the ages, comes a slightly higher creation, with sight and intelligence somewhat developed. After this the upward climb goes steadily on, until fish and ape reach the final goal in man. From man onward and upward is the intensest part of life history, for here begins the prophecy of a glorious future, together with the constant backward pull of his progenitors.

"Here, then, is the great battleground of life: animal instincts, selfishness, ferocity, over against the fine forces of spirit; the eternal struggle between the animal and the spiritual.

"There are many steps in this progress upward to man and spirit and the life immortal. What does the mollusc feel, for instance? Where does intelligence separate from instinct? Where does spirit begin? These are some of the questions of life processes.

"When the mollusc turns in its shell to seek for food; when the vertebrate begins to care for its young; when in ages upon ages a conscience appears, and a human heart begins to beat;—then the faint, first hint of the immortal life begins. All this is the preparation of unnumbered ages. Millions of years have been absorbed in the process. What, then, must be the value of the soul, if the cost be so indescribable! Yet the birth of the soul is only the beginning. Poor and weak at first, filled with evil impulse and selfish thought, it is only a shade above the animal; yet it holds the promise of immortal life!

"But just as a pugilist grows strong by hard knocks; just as courage develops from fear; just as manliness overcomes weakness, and loyalty outrides treason, and principle is born out of sin;—so the soul, through its many strifes, emerges from its base surroundings, and begins its long and evolutionary progress towards immortality.

"There are many small unseen influences at work upon the soul; for you must know that a part of every human life is beyond the seen and the mortal, and belongs to the unseen and the immortal. This is the life of the spirit which emanates from the soul.

"This organ that we call soul is invisible, for the scalpel of the surgeon has never found it, nor the eyes of the clairvoyant seen it. But it is there, invisible, and powerful for good or evil; for the soul is not always good nor always intelligent; it is educated along with the body. In the formative condition which leads to the immortal life the mind must begin its more spiritual task of creating new desires, new motives, and new activities, allowing the soul to grow out of its selfishness into unselfish service; allowing the thoughts to dwell in purer atmosphere, and life to assume a finer development.

"And thus gradually, sometimes through suffering, sometimes through loss, a few times through happiness, the soul comes into its own. Yet it arrives here as it left the earth plane; no miracle has been wrought, no immediate entrance into infinite knowledge or infinite joy. But even as the mortal slowly evolved from lower to higher, so the soul progresses onward and upward.

"How can I describe its progress? Could a butterfly tell the chrysalis of its flight? Could a bird make the creeping things of earth understand its passage through the air? Could a twentieth-century scientist make a caveman realize the wonders of electricity, of the wireless, of radium, or of the X-ray? How can one of this sphere do other than give impressions of spirit life?—vague, perhaps; indefinite, as the critics say; but still impressions; like shadows of the real, or like a chord of music that preludes faintly the harmony to follow.

"So then, having outlined the evolution of life from invisible forms to visible man, from mortal man to immortal spirit, I will leave still another impression with you of this life. But how can I give it except in phrases that you can understand? Joyous activity, increasing knowledge, loving companionship, and, finally, an ever-growing comprehension of the infinite, all-pervading Wisdom and Love."

After this message was at last completed I read it aloud one evening to F. R. He said it seemed to him good, yet he imagined the critical ones would say that, after all, the description of the unseen life was still vague and indefinite. Soon my hand gave the usual signs of wishing to write, and taking the pencil, this came from the Williams College professor:

"I have listened to the reading of Halevans' message, and know the criticism that you and others feel, that it leaves this life too vaguely described. Yet Halevans is right in saying that only impressions can be given.

"Some impressions are clearer than others, however, and I will try to give one that seems to me to present a more definite picture of this place. Will you tell me what constitutes beauty of place or scenery?"

The question surprised me; and I wondered why, when I was expecting some description of that after life, he should talk of scenery! I did not in the least guess that this question, as well as others that followed, concealed a striking illustration or argument. It was certainly not from my mind. From whose mind then? Can you tell me?

But I answered his question, that I loved the mountains, valleys, forests, rivers, etc.

"Yes," he wrote, "all these are here. But tell me what to you is the ideal scenery."

"Oh, perhaps the wild, mountain scenery, canyon, cataract, or wooded hill."

Still he persisted.

"Will you answer what appeals to you most, the wild and rugged, or the restfulness of valley or grove?"

I thought a little and answered that if I wished my soul to be startled into reverent admiration, I would choose nature's wonderlands: the Grand Canyon of the Colorado, the mighty Alps, perhaps the awe-inspiring volcano of Kilauea. Or, if I wished rest and repose, I would like the quiet valley, shady grove, or murmuring stream.

"Thus, you see," he then said, "the scenery is, to your mind, beauty as it appeals to some inner sense; and you have now given the key to heavenly beauty and surroundings. It must express some feeling or thought, if it is to represent beauty to you."

"Do you mean that it is only a thought heaven?"

"Not that exactly, but the thought or desire brings one to that which corresponds to that thought. You desire a home and the quiet places where thought may dwell. Such a home you would build, because thought forces are the creative power here. Then your soul would desire to expand and be uplifted in contemplation of grandeur, and you would go to the grandeur of mountain, sea, or sky, and lose yourself in the vastness and majesty before you. Again, in your heart of hearts, you would like the nearness of congenial companionship, and the grace and beauty of exquisitely fine surroundings, and these too would be yours. Can you get my thought at all?"

"I think you mean that the surroundings correspond to one's desires?"

"That is nearly the thought. The one word harmony might express it all."

This was all from the professor, but to my surprise, William James appeared, saying that he would like to add his testimony to what had been said of impressions of spirit life.

"Spirit is one thing," he wrote, "matter another. Do not expect to measure both in the same way. Your professor friend is trying to make your earth language convey a little more clearly the impression of the life here. We are puzzled how to get over to earth life the beauty and harmony of this one. Where all are tuned to the same vibrations, there can be no discordant notes. You are musically in tune with the great composers, and you will know what I mean when I say that to be in tune with the heavenly vibrations means a harmony undreamed on earth. It means a readjustment of the earth-born faculties. It means that the follies of earth thought are replaced by the wisdom of this sphere. It means that the wisdom of earth thought is merged in heavenly knowledge. It means that the transient loves of earth are replaced by loves and friendships so fine as to bear no resemblance to the fleeting ties of earth.

"Have I added anything to the clearness of the description?"

This was all at this time, but in closing I would like to add one more word from Professor James, who came a few evenings later with this:

"I have a word to say to earth people, if I can get it through as I wish. It is that the earth is full of mystery; every plant that grows, every wave of the ocean, every star that shines, has its own hidden mystery. Life, the life of the spirit, is God's mystery, and God's blessing, and its richest blessings are here in the unseen. Why, then, turn away from this greatest and best of all mysteries? Why not come into closer touch with this incomparably great and unseen life?"

APPENDIX

"These stories are for the mothers who have lost little children. Tell them for me, if they could know the love and tenderness that surround those little ones here, they would not grieve so much. There are many teachers here,—loving spirits, all of them,—to whom is given the care of little ones who have come to this side without their parents. The stories given here are only one of the ways in which they are cared for and educated.

DEE."

CHILDREN STORIES RECEIVED AND ARRANGED BY 'SIS'

~

IN the wave of psychic interest which has swept over the world during and since the great war, many bereaved ones have found comfort; and many believe they have received communications from their loved ones, and have become assured of future companionship in a life where war is banished and sorrow unknown. A multitude of books has appeared, many apparently inspired by those who have met the "great change," yet still can look earthward; still can tell of their passing, and their awakening in that strange new life. The soldiers who gave their all; the scholars who left their books; the great minds who have long been on that farther side;—all send some news of that spirit world, some description of its laws, occupations and interest.

Yet, one field of inquiry has been left, for the most part, vague or undescribed. This is concerning the kind of life that opens out for children, for the little ones who have passed over without their parents.

When, after many months of silence, Dee came to us, the veil between the two worlds seemed to grow transparent. At first it was enough to know that she lived,—lived with her own personality, only intensified and made more beautiful. Then we began to ask questions concerning that life and its unfoldment to her, and soon we wished to know of her occupations. One evening we asked if she could tell us of her work.

The reply came quickly:

"Can you believe that I am developing into a teacher?"

'We surely can,' we replied, 'but will you tell us just how and what you are teaching?'

"I am teaching little children at present, and love the work. I tell them stories that have a lesson in them."

'Something like kindergarten work?'

"Yes; and I love it; for the children are so quick to learn, and so loving, too. I like to mother the little things, so that they may not miss too much the care and tenderness of the mother left on earth."

'Can you give us some idea of the way you teach them?'

"I will try. Today it was in this way:

"'Once upon a time', I told them, 'there was a beautiful fairy who took little children to a wonderful garden where they could play. Then the fairy told them of a new game.' And here I tell it to them, pretending to quote the fairy's words. And so I draw them into all sorts of little, new, educational thoughts, by clothing the thought in a story.

"Sometimes I describe animals on earth, and they are much interested because they have never seen them here. You would laugh to see me trying to represent lions and tigers. But I do not tell them they would harm little children, because evil is not known to them. No thought of cruelty must be allowed to enter their minds."

This description of her work made us wish to hear more, and one evening she gave us the following:

"My children are always the dearest work that I have, and I hope that I shall never stop teaching them. Would you like to hear about today's lesson?

"I wished to tell them a story of activity in work; so I described the little things of earth, like the ants and bees and other busy little creatures. The children wanted to know what they were like and I tried to tell them. But I could not quite make them understand. Then I tried to make pictures of them, but as I am no artist, that was not much better. So I finally said that the ants crawl and the bees fly. Then immediately we had a crawling, flying crowd of children that completely overwhelmed their teacher, and she called a halt to the lesson and joined in the fun!"

Again, when we asked for a "kindergarten" story, she told us the following:

"Today I called a tiny child to come to me, and when I had her in my arms, I placed my hand on her head and said to the other children: 'Now this, where my hand is, is a beautiful house that we are going to furnish, and you may tell me what we should put in it'. One said, 'There must be a big room full of love', opening her arms as if she would enclose the universe. Another declared that we must put in kind thoughts for other children who had no mothers here. Another said we could 'make a playroom in the house, and play games, and see pictures of all those queer animals on earth'. Another thought, 'We might have a little mother's room, where we could mother other little children as you mother us'. I said, 'Do you think the rooms in this beautiful house are all filled now?' One replied, 'Wouldn't love fill all the others?' 'Pretty near it', I said, 'but how about truth and knowledge and growth?' 'Why, each of these could have a room, too', they said. And the little child in my arms began to feel of her head to find where all these rooms could be."

We asked once if she did not have many children come to her who had been wrongly taught, or not at all, and therefore had only false ideas and impressions. My pencil wrote:

"Most of them leave their false impressions with their bodies. One of the children here was a child of criminal parents, and came over poisoned by wrong teaching; but the influence here was so good and so gentle that she soon outgrew the other impressions. I think she would have drifted into a criminal life if she had been left on earth; here, she is very dear and good."

'If every child had been surrounded by right influences, what would have happened?'

"Most of them would have been good, I think; and their influence over the actually bad would have held evil actions in check."

The work of my life nearly always has been in music, and the part of it that I have liked best has been the direction of choruses and choirs; yet I was greatly surprised when Dee on that unseen side drew a lesson from even this circumstance.

"Can you guess what I talked to my children about today?" she wrote one evening. "I told them that you were my friend on earth, and I told them how you loved music. Then they wanted to try to sing, and I wish you could have heard them. They made many sweet sounds, but no time and no harmony. Then I described how you used to beat time to have us sing together. Then they all tried that. I thought they were very dear, trying to follow my motions and keep together.

"The lesson was, of course, unity in action, and that to work together in harmony meant better and bigger things than for each to try separately. I think the idea appealed to them and increased their desire for united and harmonious action."

"I do so love the work with the children, and their quick responsiveness to my thought. I am teaching them about unselfishness now, and how to send their thoughts out to others in kindness and love. Sometimes a newly arrived child feels desolate and lonely without the sheltering protection of a mother's arms. Then the children can be of the greatest service in surrounding the little one with love and tender thought. There are many ways in which children can learn the true office of unselfishness and love, and their gentle and loving attentions to others react upon themselves in added happiness.

"I wish you could see them, all so dainty and light and beautiful. Today we walked in the garden looking at the flowers. Then we tried to find the colors that each liked best, and each picked out her favorite color. One chose a pink flower, and said that was for love. Another chose white, because that to her was like the baby angels. Another gathered purple flowers because her mother had loved that color. Dearest of all was the little blue flower that stood for hope and happiness, they said. And so we went through the garden, picking flowers and telling what they meant, until we had nearly all the virtues represented, but no faults. When I asked where the faults were, they said, 'Why, flowers have no faults'. Then I called them my flowers, and told them that they, too, must be without faults if they would belong in the beautiful garden of love.

"Ah, dear mothers of little children, I wish you could see these happy ones at play in these wonderful gardens! Can you not think of them so, rather than taken from you and borne to some far-away unknown place?"

Then after a while came a serious story: "Many years ago a boy told his mother that he was going to be a great man, and that he would have riches and power, and make others do as he wished. Well, the years went by, and the boy grew to manhood, and he did attain power and riches and the gift of controlling others; but in far, far different ways from his own boyish plans. He did have power, but power born out of suffering and disappointment. He did have riches, the riches of a spirit made pure by loss. And he did control others, through the power of love and sympathy. For poverty, ill-health and disappointment had come to him in so many different ways, that his pride was turned into humility, his selfishness into kindness, and all his character into true nobility. Thus he was given his desires, but in ways he could not have dreamed, and with results he never anticipated. And so, I tried to show the children that sorrow and disappointment to earthly lives are often heavenly gifts."

The following story rather reflects on the writer, but I think I will include it just the same:

"I will tell you about my children today. I have talked of you many times,—of your music, of our friendship, of our many happy times together; and today they asked me to tell them more about that friend on earth. I told them she was very dear, but sometimes she could not understand what I was trying to tell her, and then she got cross! They asked me what 'cross' meant. Then I tried to scowl and wrinkle up my face, and I wish you could have heard them laugh! So I had to explain that you were grieved sometimes, just as they were grieved when they wanted their parents to see them, and the parents could not see nor understand. So then they got quite sorry for my little friend.

"I just wanted to show them how much you were in my thought, and show you how my little pupils are growing to think of you, too."

Some evenings later this came:

"I told my children today that I would talk a little about history. They did not know the word and asked what it meant. I said it meant the stories of the lives of people, and the places in which they lived. But I soon got beyond my depth and had to call for help. I called a teacher of history from another plane, and he began in such simple and beautiful ways to tell of lives on different planets and the things that happened there, that I learned not only the history, but his beautiful manner of telling it; and I will study with him to get more knowledge and better ways of expressing that knowledge."

Here her writing stopped, but after a little, Mary took the pencil and wrote:

"She has not told it all, for he said some things of her teaching that were lovely to hear. You see, she is so loving that she teaches the children that the greatest thing of all is love, and that love is the foundation of all that is good in character and life, and they grow into such expression of it that they are more than ordinarily beautiful in character and appearance, for character expresses itself outwardly in the appearance."

We have been so curious about the blending of story and instruction that we repeat our request for the daily teachings quite often. This one came in answer to one such request:

"I had a little hide-and-seek story for them today. I don't like to preach about character; so I turn the preaching into playing, and this time I described the old game of hide-and-seek to them, and how we shouted 'I spy' when the hidden person was found. Then I told them of the little thoughts that hid away, and that now I was going to try to find them. The children grew interested and bright eyes were following mine in the pretended search,—for, really, I could see the characters written on the souls before me. Sometimes I saw helpfulness; sometimes a kind thought that seemed to blossom out like a flower; and again, just love illumined the soul. Such dear thoughts in nearly all! I hardly know if they had any real faults, only beginnings of what might become so. Now and then a shade of self-love, or maybe a tiny grain of selfishness or pride, but all so small as scarcely to be called faults. But I said 'I spy' just the same, and told them what I saw, and said we must drive them out and chase them away before they grew into faults. So then we played we had them on the run, and chased them hither and yon, until I think we drove them all away. And everyone laughed and was happy, but the lesson remained."

Once when we asked for Dee, Mary told us she was with her children, but that she would call her. When she came, she told us the story-lesson she had just been giving.

"We were trying to learn about the stars, and I told them about the planet Mars, and they wanted to go there at once. I told them of the study they must first have, and they wanted a lesson right away. What could I do but tell them about travel of all kinds:—on earth, in the clouds, by land and by water, by material and by spiritual ways. They listened so eagerly that I could not find it in my heart to tell them that years must elapse before they would be wise enough to travel to planets where were conditions so different from here. So I told them a fairy story about travel, and we all journeyed together in fairy boats with fairy sails, up above the stars, and swung on comets, and danced through northern lights, and played with elves and goblins, and finally slid down a moonbeam to our home here once more.

"That was just as Mary called me, and I ran away and escaped further questions; and wasn't I glad I—"

But Mary added:

"The children are not going to stop there, though, and her troubles are not over yet."

To which Dee responded:

"We will dodge the whole subject next time by starting on something entirely new."

When we read this story aloud later, the following was added:

"My fairy story was not as perfect a success as I hoped, for the children still insist on seeing a real planet! I have had to describe the earth to them, and let them take that as a model for the others. The things I can't exactly get around on that dark planet, are the sin, suffering, ignorance, and selfishness, the fierce wild animals, and the dangers that lurk in hidden places. Could you describe the life on earth and keep it all within the limit of love, wisdom, and goodness?"

'No, I am afraid not. Can you?'

"I am telling a rather one-sided story at present, leaving out the dark side, hoping no embarrassing questions will be asked until the little ones grow older and wiser."

"I have been telling my children about the little men and women of another universe,—a story that a friend told me after one of her far-away visits. We know something of other universes; but have to depend upon our teachers, or those who have been there, for definite knowledge, because we have not taken up the studies that would help us to go there.

"Well, my friend told us that, among the planets of one of the great suns, was one where life was very minute, and the children were fairy-like in stature. Perhaps they could not use a rose leaf for a couch, but might sleep under the branches. The children were so delighted that they wanted to go there at once. Then I told them of the studies and the years of experience and knowledge that must be acquired before they could go, and they turned to their studies very eagerly, believing these would lead them to this fairy-like world; while I thought nothing could be more fairy-like than this dainty group of children."

One evening we had been talking with several friends through the pencil. Finally Dee took it and wrote:

"I am tired of being shut out, and have concluded to step in. Will you take a story to-night? I have taught the children a new game. It had no special moral, but it kept them busy and happy.

"We were trying to see the colors in a rainbow. I mean a spiritual rainbow, for we do not see earth colors. This was as far as we got, when one of the little ones said: 'Could we break it up into dresses?' and another said: 'No, let's play it is a beautiful chariot for us to ride in.'

"They knew about chariots in other stories. So we all jumped into the rainbow and sailed around, or played we did, and told what we saw. Some saw moons and stars; some saw other little playmates coming out of the sky to play with them; some laughed at the queer animals they conjured up; and we had a laughing, happy group. Then suddenly one little girl said: 'I want my mama. Where is she?' For the little thing had come over alone. So we stopped our play, and all began comforting the child and leading her into happy thought.

"So, after all, the little game ended in sympathy and service. So don't you think it was a lesson, after all?"

"You might be able to take a story today. Will you try?

"Imagine the tiny forms moving about, as dainty as flowers, and as light and airy as butterflies. I cannot describe them well, nor their motions; but all are full of grace and beauty. Today I was trying to tell them of—"

"Will you try not to think out the story. I am telling it, not you!"

I had not realized that my own thought was interfering; but I said: "All right, go ahead."

"I will write if you will stop thinking. Will you write what I wish? I was trying to say 'figures', but you would not write it."

'I thought the word came from my own mind. I did not think you would be telling of figures there.'

"We do tell them of figures, and give them some idea of numbers, too. We have to begin with the elementary things, as with earth children; and through them lead up to higher things. So I was trying to teach them to count. And because they got mixed up in the names of the figures, I had them form in a little dance, where each one was a figure. And I had them moving in pretty ways, each answering to the name of a number. Sometimes they got mixed up, but the laugh only added to the pleasure of the play. And finally they learned to count very well to a certain number."

'Did they learn up to a hundred?'

"Million would be better."

'A million!'

"Yes. What do you expect of little ones with spirit intelligence? You are comparing them to earth children. Here they learn millions as quickly as those of earth would learn tens or hundreds."

'How long have you been teaching the class?'

"I have been with them as teacher almost since I gained my spiritual sight and hearing."

'I suppose some have graduated from your class before this?'

"Yes; many have gone on into higher classes. But I teach the tiny ones still, and many others are coming from the earth plane, so that I always have many to teach."

'Can you tell us how many are in your charge?'

"The number changes, as some move on and others come in. But there are very many; you would call them hundreds."

'Do you teach them in separate classes?'

"I take them in different classes at times, but many times have them all together."

'We were interested the other day when you told of the one who was homesick for her mother.'

"Some are bewildered at first, and call often for their mothers. But the love and tenderness that is here soon help them to be happy, and wait for their earth parents with love in their hearts for those who loved them from the first."

"Will you take a story to-night about my children?

"They were today trying to see pictures of life on earth. Some of them have to do with war and other troubles, and I have had a hard time trying to explain that these things existed in the planet they came from.

"They could not understand, and one little one said, 'Why, what was love doing all this time?' I said I thought love must have hid her eyes and gone away for a time. Then one of them put her hands to her eyes, and the others pretended to quarrel and have a little war, and before I knew it a game was started. But love,—the little one who pretended to be love,—took her hands away from her eyes and smiled. And such a smile! Did you ever see the sun come out of a dark cloud? Well, she smiled just such a smile, and the children all ran to her and circled about her and the war was over.

"Don't you think that might happen on earth if there were love enough?"

'If only there were love enough!'

"You must just go on trying to teach the world of better things. It will be long before selfishness is changed into service, but it must come sooner or later."

The End

www.ingramcontent.com/pod-product-compliance
Lightning Source LLC
Chambersburg PA
CBHW030824090426
42737CB00009B/870